Just Like Glass

Just Like Glass

A Family Memoir

Amy Wight Chapman

Amy Wight Chapman

with Steve Wight, Greg Wight,
Andy Wight, and Leslie Wight Grenier

MUSEUMS OF THE
BETHEL HISTORICAL SOCIETY
Bethel, Maine

Published by the Museums of the Bethel Historical Society, Bethel, Maine

"Prologue" originally appeared in *Down East: The Magazine of Maine*, June 2014, as "Just Like Glass."

Leo Dangel, "In Memoriam" from *Saving Singletrees.* Copyright © WSC Press, 2013. Reprinted with permission.

Edna St. Vincent Millay, "The courage that my mother had" from Collected Poems. Copyright 1954, © 1982 by Norma Millay Ellis. Reprinted with the permission of The Permissions Company, LLC on behalf of Holly Peppe, Literary Executor, The Millay Society, www.millay.org.

Cover design by Donna Funteral

Kintsugi is the Japanese art of repairing broken pottery with lacquer mixed with precious metals, turning the repair into a beautiful and integral part of the finished piece.

ISBN: 978-0-9614153-9-6

For Steve, Greg, Andy, and Leslie,

who lived this story,

and

in memory of my sister-in-law Peggy,

our Best Big Sister Ever

Preface

"It's a lovely idea," said our instructor, a writer I greatly admire. "But it's not a memoir.

It was a Saturday morning in February of 2011, and two dozen would-be memoir writers were gathered in the basement meeting room at the Norway Memorial Library for the first of two sessions of "Memoir Boot Camp." I had just pitched my idea for the essay I would write about my mother.

"I want to write it from her point of view, in the first person," I had said. I went on to describe the book I hoped to write eventually—the story of my mother's life, focusing on the year before my birth, and told in her own voice.

I didn't want to break any rules—I wasn't even sure what the rules of memoir were, and I was there to learn—so I did a quick pivot. I wrote an essay about something else entirely for that workshop, and since then I have written many personal essays from my own point of view, as well as short stories, blog posts, and a weekly column for my local paper.

But the idea for this book never left me, nor did the conviction that it needed to be written in my mother's voice. So I decided to write it, whether it could be neatly categorized on a bookshelf or not.

I invited my four siblings into the project, and their enthusiasm was gratifying, especially considering that I was presuming to write about a time they had all lived through and I hadn't. I emailed them questions, prompting a flurry of shared memories, many of which I incorporated into the story.

I originally planned to use my siblings' input for a combination of inspiration, added detail, and fact-checking. I would write the book from my mother's point of view, basing it on what I knew about that year in her life from things she had told me, the memories of my brothers and sister, and a lot of poetic license. And because I would be, of necessity, making up a lot of things, as my mother used to say, "out of whole cloth," I would call it a novel, rather than a memoir.

Writing in my mother's voice was surprisingly easy. Having been born nearly a decade after the last of my siblings, in some ways I was raised as the only child of a single parent, and my mother and I knew each other well.

By the time I was old enough to have real conversations with her, I suppose that the sharp trauma of my father's sudden death had been dulled somewhat, and because I had not lived through it myself, I never felt the same reluctance to bring the subject up that my siblings did.

Late in the project, though, I began to realize that I wanted to include more than just my brothers' and sister's memories, told as secondhand (or even thirdhand) experiences. Their own stories, told in their own words, with their own individual voices coming through loud and clear, added more depth and substance than I could have imagined.

It's a testament to the trust and the bond the five of us share that when I asked them for permission to use their words, their responses were immediate and nearly identical: "Of course you can."

My gratitude to them is boundless, and my heart is full.

Here is the short explanation of the voices you'll hear in *Just Like Glass:* the words of my mother, Ruth, are mine, as are the prologue and a few other short essays in my own voice. The excerpts from my grandfather's diaries are exactly as he wrote them.

And the voices of my siblings—Steve, Greg, Andy, and Leslie—are their own. I've combined their answers from many different interviews—usually conducted by email, since the times when we are all together in one place are regrettably rare—and, in a few cases, rearranged a few words or phrases to clarify meaning, but the voices, the memories, and the emotions are all theirs.

In the end, the book that had all along felt more like a memoir than a novel to me, despite the fact that it was my mother's story and not my own, truly became what I finally decided to call it: a family memoir.

Prologue

Amy

IN 1954, MY PARENTS BOUGHT A lakefront lot in western Maine for two hundred dollars, cleared and leveled a building site, and began, with the help of their four kids, ages four to ten, to build what we have always called "camp." It was never meant to be a "cottage" or a "lake house"; it was just "camp," with exposed rafters and tiny bedrooms and an open loft full of lumpy beds.

My father had grown up in Bethel, a few miles away. He was an avid outdoorsman, a Scout leader, a rockhound, and a hiker, who always knew that his exile to Connecticut and New Jersey was only temporary. Like so many young Mainers of the 1930s and '40s, he had left the state after college to seek his fortune, and exile was the price he paid to profit from his engineering degree.

As soon as school let out, my mother and the kids were installed at camp for the summer, and my father joined them there on weekends, and for his annual vacation. It was always understood that when he retired, my parents would spend summers at the lake, and winters in a small, tidy home they would buy or build "on a hill in Bethel."

Then, in 1958, just as the school year was wrapping up and the kids were itching to get to camp, my father had a heart attack. My mother remembered thinking, when he came home from work that day and went straight to bed, that it was the first time she had ever known him to be ill. A short time later, he called her upstairs. "When I got there, he just...died," she told me, many years later.

My mother was thirty-eight years old. She had four grief-stricken children, now aged eight to fourteen, and when the funeral was over, she put them in the station wagon with the family dog and drove from New Jersey to Maine to spend the summer at camp, because that was what they had planned, and she couldn't think of what else to do.

I sit here on the deck now and look out at the lake and wonder how on earth she found the strength to come here that summer, to make the beds and open the windows and clean out the mouse droppings, to just keep on getting out of bed in the morning, let alone the strength to feed and nurture four kids, and supervise the completion of the camp over the next few summers. (In later years, if anyone commented about its somewhat quirky construction, she would say, "Well, what do you expect? It was built by teenagers!")

By mid-summer, my mother began to suspect something, and by summer's end she knew: she was pregnant.

I was born early the following March, and in June, as always, the family came to camp. My mother laid me on my stomach on a blanket in the middle of the big oak dining table, where I could raise my head and look out the window at the lake. It was my first summer at camp.

Connecticut, where the family moved that year from New Jersey, was where we went to school, and where, later, my mother worked as a school librarian. We had friends in Connecticut, and all the usual growing-up things took place there, but we all knew that our real lives happened at camp.

Every June, when we turned off the main road and onto the dirt road to camp, we had to throw open the car door to let our cocker spaniel, Lucky, leap out and run the last mile beside the station wagon; otherwise, he would pitch an absolute fit, clawing our legs bloody as he tried to jump out the window. If it could have gotten us there a moment sooner, we would all have run along with him.

My mother spent fifty summers at camp, and there was never a summer morning that she didn't rise early and look out at the lake, to see if it was steaming, or choppy, or smooth. If there was no wind to stir the surface, she would tell people, "When I got up this morning, the lake was just like glass."

She held both hands out in front of her, flat, palms down, and said it—always, for fifty years, with the same hint of awe and amazement—"Just like glass."

In the early afternoon my mother
was doing the dishes. I climbed
onto the kitchen table, I suppose
to play, and fell asleep there.
I was drowsy and awake, though,
as she lifted me up, carried me
on her arms into the living room,
and placed me on the davenport,
but I pretended to be asleep
the whole time, enjoying the luxury—
I was too big for such a privilege
and just old enough to form
my only memory of her carrying me.
She's still moving me to a softer place.

—Leo Dangel, "In Memoriam"

June 20, 1959, Kittery, Maine

Ruth

Off to Maine — Andy ties load

TRAFFIC IS LIGHT AS WE APPROACH THE tall green bridge over the Piscataqua River. It's barely noon; we got away even earlier than I could have hoped. The older kids were a big help, packing the car last night in the dark and up before dawn so we could get on the road in good season.

We ate cold cereal standing up in the kitchen, and I washed our dishes while the kids packed a few things into a cooler—a quart of milk, half a dozen eggs, some juice—and found a space for it in the back of the station wagon. Andy walked the dog. Winnie padded out of her rented room at the back of the house in her robe and slippers to say goodbye, then we crammed ourselves into the car.

Amy's car bed is wedged in the back seat between two of the kids. She's been awake, but quiet and watchful, for most of the trip. The others have all taken turns riding up front with me—the favorite seat—and squeezed in the way-back with our gear—the least favorite. There has been no complaining, not even when I had to pull over again—barely ten minutes after we'd left the Massachusetts highway rest stop where we'd stretched our legs and walked the dog—to change the baby's reeking diaper.

This summer will be a better one than last. Not "normal," whatever that means, because I know at the very center of my gut that nothing in my life can ever be normal now. But the ways in which this summer will be different will not be the ways in which last summer was different, and I am grateful for that. I am grateful for the baby, for the new house to which we'll return at the end of August. And for time, which, though it does not heal sorrow, does, quite effectively, blunt it.

A year ago, when I could sleep—which was only every third night or so—waking in the morning was like wrenching a bandage from an unhealed wound, feeling the scab ripped away from the raw flesh. Now that scar, though I imagine it still ragged and uneven and pink, is beginning to whiten. While I know it will never become a seamless part of me, I will not always have to move, and speak, and think in certain, cautious ways to avoid knocking against it and bringing back the searing pain.

June 16, 1958, Westfield, New Jersey
Ruth

IT WAS A MONDAY, THAT EVENING THAT Bill died, and I had taken the boys to their Scout meeting. Bill, who was their troop's assistant Scoutmaster, was supposed to take them, of course, but he had come home ill from his business trip to New York City, had gone immediately upstairs to lie down. I didn't know how to react to that, simply because I had never once known him to be sick enough to go to bed, not in all of our seventeen years together. It was one of the things we had in common, one of the things I appreciated about him—that, like me, he was neither delicate nor a hypochondriac. If we had a cold, or a headache, or a strained back, we took an aspirin and went about our usual business. It was how we got things done.

But this was something different. It felt like terrible heartburn, he said. Must have been something he ate. Actually, he admitted, he had felt a little off over the weekend, too. Not bad like this—just a dull ache under his breastbone, like the mild heartburn he'd had from time to time, though he'd rarely mentioned that to me—but today, in the city and on the train home, it had gotten worse. He'd be fine, he said, but he guessed I'd have to drive the boys to Scouts. Tell them to explain to Mr. Fish that he wasn't feeling well this evening, but he'd be in touch with him tomorrow. They'd go over the plans for the upcoming camping trip—a week of work, clearing brush and making trails, at Sabattis Wilderness Camp in the Adirondacks—then. I shouldn't worry.

And I wasn't worried, not really. I was surprised and perhaps, I suppose, a little bit put out, because I'd been looking forward to a quiet evening at home. Grammy—Bill's mother, Lena—had gone to her room right after we ate, as she often did, and she would call me shortly to help her undress for bed. Leslie was down the street at her friend Diana's; she'd gone there after school and stayed for dinner, and I had been about to walk down to retrieve her. I would have reminded her that tomorrow was her very last day of third grade, and hustled her off to bed, too, so I could have the house to myself for an hour or two. Then I'd have sat in the living room with my knitting, turning on only the lamp beside my chair, savoring the quiet and the one small circle of light in the darkening house.

Instead, I drove the boys to their meeting, and told them I'd be back to pick them up in two hours. I had only just returned home and shut the side door behind me when I heard Bill calling my name from upstairs. I don't know if he had been calling to me for a minute, for ten minutes or fifteen, or if he started to call only when he heard me come in. In any case, I heard my name once as I crossed the kitchen, pausing to drop my purse on the counter beside the stove, again when I was halfway up the stairs, and a third time as I pushed through the half-open bedroom door.

The sun hadn't even begun to go down, and the light coming through the windows was clear and yellow, not the diffused salmon-pink light of sunset that would wash the room later, as I waited there, after the doctor came, for the men from the funeral home. In the strong sunlight that still fell across the bed, Bill's face was the color of ashes. His cheeks, forehead, and lips—even his eyes when he opened them and looked at me—they were all the same flat gray. His jaw was clenched and his fists gripped handfuls of the sheet under which he lay, the blanket and spread kicked to the floor. His lips were moving, still forming my name, but no sound came out.

I suppose he had used up all the strength he had, waiting stubbornly until I was there with him to give in, to draw one last wretched breath. There were no final words, no nuggets of wisdom I could pass on to our children, no instructions for me on how to begin living this other life. There was just a slackening of the clenched jaw, a flutter of the eyelids before they remained closed.

I'm sure I called his name, over and over again, but I knew, even as I pulled the sheet from the loosening grip of his fingers and laid my head on his chest, that there would be no heartbeat to hear. I stood up then and tried to think.

A doctor. I needed to call a doctor. Not because I thought there was anything that could be done to change the fact that Bill was dead; I knew there wasn't. But without a doctor, this would be considered an "unattended death"—there would be an investigation, a medical examiner, perhaps even the police. I had less than two hours before the boys' Scout meeting would end, and even if I could stall Leslie's return from Diana's, it wouldn't be for long. I thought about them arriving home to find police cars in the driveway. There was a directory beneath the heavy black phone on the bedside table, and I found our family physician's home number and dialed it.

I don't remember what I said to Dr. Hatch's wife when she answered, but she quickly put the doctor on the line, and I explained things as well as I could. He lived only a few blocks away, and he was there in minutes, not bothering to knock or ring the doorbell, but entering through the side door into the kitchen and racing up the stairs, calling to me.

I was sitting on the edge of the bed, holding Bill's hand. I wasn't crying. I couldn't cry yet; I knew that. If I started to cry, I might never stop, and there were so many things to be done before I allowed that to happen.

The doctor performed a brief examination, then drew a pen and notebook from his bag and, glancing at his wristwatch, made a few notes. When he turned his attention to me, his face was sad and kind. "Let me make some calls for you," he said. And, "Where are the children?" And, "Who can I call to stay with you?"

It was then that I remembered Grammy, downstairs in her bedroom. "My mother-in-law is here. I haven't told her yet," I told the doctor. "She's in a wheelchair," I added, as though this would explain my forgetting her presence altogether. "I need to help her get ready for bed."

I went down to see to Grammy. She was sitting beside her window, her knobby fingers clutching the sill, straining forward in her chair. "Who's here?" she asked sharply, half turning her body toward me as I entered her room. "Whose car is in the driveway? I heard Bill calling to you. Why didn't he take the boys to Scouts?"

I don't recall the words I used to tell her that her only son was dead. I don't remember what she said, either, but I remember that she lifted her arms to me and I leaned down to her, and we held onto each other as long minutes passed. Her thin hands patted my back and, for the first time in twenty-eight years, for just a moment, I felt mothered. I pulled away, and she looked up at me, tears caught in the deep lines of her face.

"Ruth," she whispered. "What are we going to do?" and, as quickly as that, I was once again the one in charge, although I didn't have any answers.

The doctor called the funeral home, and the minister from our church. He asked again, "Who can I call to stay with you?"

I didn't want anyone. Soon enough, my children would be home. I wanted nothing more than to draw the five of us into a tight circle, to shut out this world gone suddenly senseless, to let it spin and pitch out of control beyond the fortress of our rigid backs.

But Dr. Hatch was insistent, and I tried to think of someone—a neighbor, a friend from church—who wouldn't be busy with her own family. On this Monday evening before the last day of school, just after sunset, when children had been called inside for their baths and husbands were relaxing with the paper, I knew just what every woman up and down our street was doing. They were folding laundry snatched from the line before it was dampened by dew, ironing shirts and blouses to be worn to work and school the next morning, wrapping cookies and peanut-butter sandwiches in waxed paper for tomorrow's lunches.

Finally, I thought of Winnie, who was the associate director of Christian education at our church. Although we weren't especially close, she had been to the house several times. Because she had no family of her own, we, like other families in the church, had occasionally invited her to have Sunday dinner with us. Middle-aged, lonely, with her own history of heartache, she would be willing, even eager, to drop everything and come right over.

So Dr. Hatch called Winnie. He called Diana's parents, told them what had happened, asked them to keep Leslie a little longer, said someone would be along as soon as possible to walk her home. He promised to stop at the church, where the boys were at their Scout meeting, and ask Mr. Fish to bring them home, but, please, to delay returning as long as he could. "But Greg has a math test tomorrow," I said, hearing how foolish the words sounded even as I spoke them. "He'll want to get right home to study."

I told him I'd be all right, that he could go, but the doctor stayed until Winnie arrived, then the men from the funeral home. I think there was some paperwork, some forms I had to sign, but I don't remember what they were. Winnie cried and hugged me and wanted me to sit down and drink a cup of tea, but I told her there was too much to do.

The minister came, and he sat with me beside the bed and prayed, a long, rambling prayer that I'm sure was full of reassurances and promises of Heaven, things meant to make me feel at peace, but I couldn't pay attention to his words. I was thinking that I needed to call Bill's supervisor at work before it got too late in the evening, and his sister in Texas. I wished I had a pen and notepad, so I could write down these things I thought of as the minister prayed, then, later, cross them off as I did them, just so I'd be sure, tomorrow, that I had.

The two men from Gray's Funeral Home leaned a collapsed aluminum gurney carefully against the wall of the upstairs hall, taking pains not to let it scratch. They stood, quiet and respectful, outside the open bedroom door until the minister was finished, almost fading into the dim light and the striped wallpaper behind them. They wore dark suits and ties and identical white shirts, and were perhaps ten or fifteen years older than I, with graying dark hair and kindly lined faces. When they entered the bedroom, they both paused in front of me and looked into my eyes for a moment as they murmured that they were sorry for my loss.

Reverend McCorison offered me his arm, and I took it as we followed the gurney down the stairs and out through the front door. I leaned against him as we stood together on the front step. I was relieved to see that none of the neighbors had come out of their houses to watch, though I was sure I saw the curtains move in the front window of the Glassmans' house across the street.

The men from the funeral home had backed their long black car across the lawn, fitting it neatly between the flowerbeds that ran the length of the walk, careful to keep all four tires on the flagstone path. It was nearly full dark by then, and a dim light spilled from the open rear door of the car. They slid the gurney with Bill's body, covered by a dark cloth, expertly onto the rails attached to the inside walls of the car and I heard it click into place. There was a second click as one of the men shut the rear door as quietly as he could.

The car bumped gently over the low curb and onto the street, and I watched until it was out of sight. The sky was a dark purple velvet, no moon in sight. Venus hung low on the horizon to the west, and soon the first pinpricks of stars would begin to show themselves. I strained my eyes, watching, waiting to wish on the first one to appear.

Before I could make out the first star, a meteor streaked across the sky. That would do. Quickly, I squeezed my eyes shut and wished hard. I didn't waste my wish by asking for the impossible, for things to be undone. I didn't wish for good health, as I often did, or for money, even though it had already occurred to me that we might soon be in dire straits. Without needing to think about it twice, I wished for the thing I knew I would need most: courage.

The minister's hand between my shoulder blades guided me back inside. I wanted to ask him where he thought Bill was now, but I was afraid he might not understand what I meant. I wasn't sure myself. Bill might be in that long dark car with his body, or upstairs in the bedroom where I had stood, leaning over him as he died. Or he might not be anywhere at all.

I sat down on the couch to wait for the boys to get home, trying to think of what to say when they did, knowing they would recall these first words exactly, hearing them over and over, for the rest of their lives. After nearly three decades, my own father's bleak pronouncement—"Your mother is dead"—still played in a continuous loop behind the layers of memory and thought that masked but never fully erased his words.

So I thought hard about what to say to the boys. But when Mr. Fish's car pulled into the driveway, I was in the small bathroom off the kitchen, where I had gone because I thought I might throw up, and because it was the one place where Winnie wouldn't follow me, and where, if I let the water run, full force, in the sink, I couldn't hear Grammy's reedy voice calling my name. I stepped out into the kitchen in time to hear Reverend McCorison's voice from the side door. "Boys," he was saying to my babies, in the same sonorous tone he used from the pulpit on Sundays, "the time has come for you to become men. Your father has died."

"Boys to men in a heartbeat"

Steve, Greg, Andy, Leslie

Andy: We don't do death well in our family. I mean, we had so little experience with death of close relatives that in 1958 we were all in shock when Dad so suddenly dropped dead. There had been a little very quiet talk about untimely death in our house because a man in the church about Dad's age had died suddenly about a month before he did. There was talk about not much planning or insurance and then—wham—it happened to us.

Leslie: On the evening Dad died I was at my friend Diana Sweet's house down the street for supper. I remember that we had warm red junket rennet custard for dessert—weird how details stick with me. Afterwards Diana's father set up the movie projector and we watched home movies. We were all laughing and having a great time, running the movies in forward and reverse, when the phone rang. Mrs. Sweet called Mr. Sweet into the kitchen for a couple minutes. Mrs. Sweet said it was Mom who called, and I could stay a while longer. That made me happy, because we were having so much fun. The parents became very somber; they put the movies back on, but would not run them backwards or joke around anymore. It seemed odd to me, but I didn't question it.

After a while, the doorbell rang, and Winnie was there to pick me up. That seemed very weird! When we got home, Mom, the boys, and the minister were all sitting around the living room, looking grim and not saying a word. When I asked what was going on, Mom said two words: "Daddy died."

Poor Mom had just dealt with breaking the news to the boys and then she had to go through it all over again with her sobbing, heartbroken daughter. I remember telling her I had a stomach-ache, and she said, "It's probably because of this thing." Thing??? This was the most devastating day of my life!

Greg: Dad had been on a business trip; he was to take us three boys to Scouts that evening, but Mom took us instead. I had to get right home to study for a math exam. I distinctly recall someone whispering to our Scoutmaster, Mr. Fish, and him saying explosively, "NO!"

At the end of the meeting, he suggested we boys go with him to a cabin the Scouts owned not too far away to collect some equipment. My protests that I had to get home to study were overridden.

Andy: The bogus trip to that Scout cabin was to "find" some equipment we had left there. The whole thing didn't feel right to me at the time—totally out of character for our very organized Scoutmaster.

Steve: My recollection was that Dad was in New York City with other coworkers on a single-day business trip. He came home sick and went right to bed. Mom did take us to Scouts, and we were taken on a time-stalling trip (this is where Greg's details fascinate me).

I don't know whether he was already dead when she returned from taking us to Scouts, but she called a doctor who attempted to revive him using chest compressions without success. The equipment-gathering ruse Greg describes was to give the funeral home time to remove the body.

Greg: When we eventually got out of Mr. Fish's car at home, we saw a lot of cars in the drive, so we ran around to the back door, where we were met by the minister who uttered the line that quite probably altered my life more than any other before or since—and not in a good way: "Boys, the time has come for you to become men. Your father has died."

Steve: I do remember being told that I was now "the man of the house," and I remember saying that we would have to sell the camp. Mom stated firmly that the camp was central to the family—and I suspect she meant also to her relationship with Dad—and that we would keep it at all costs.

Andy: I totally remember and have reacted all of my life to the minister's words. Steve, I know you acted like the man of the house, but really the words were spoken to all three of us. Boys to men in a heartbeat...

1941–1942, Connecticut

Ruth

IN THE SUMMER OF 1941, WHEN I FIRST met Bill, I was newly graduated from college with a degree—of rather dubious practical value—in English. Unlike many of the girls in my class, I had not—somewhat to my father's consternation, I suppose—gotten married, or even engaged, during my four years at the University of Maine. In fact, although there was a boy who wanted to marry me, I was disinclined, and not at all sorry to put some space between us. So, just a week after graduation, I arrived in Hartford, Connecticut, moved into the YMCA, where some friends and I had gotten rooms, and went to work for the Aetna Insurance Company.

Despite our bravado, we Maine girls found Hartford a daunting place, filled with hard-edged girls and slick city boys. When it came to socializing, we were most comfortable in a group of our own kind. It wasn't long before a couple of my girlfriends met a group of boys who'd come down from Maine to seek their fortune in the production of aircraft, ships, and other military goods.

Though it would be six more months before the attack on Pearl Harbor would send many of those same boys into uniform and overseas, these industries were already burgeoning in support of the war efforts of the European Allies. The jobs they provided were a lucrative alternative to the spotty work available back home, where rural areas were slow to get the message that the Great Depression had finally lifted.

The boys were staying in a rundown camp they'd rented on Hitchcock Lake and commuting to jobs in places like the Waterbury brass companies or the aircraft and machine tool plants in the Hartford area. With summer in full swing, one July weekend someone proposed an "old-fashioned picnic" at the lake, and the whole gang of us girls threw ourselves into preparing baskets full of sandwiches and fried chicken and brownies and lemonade, to save the poor boys from what we imagined was their monotonous diet of canned beans and beer.

Bill was one of the boys, though a few years older than most of the others. He had worked his way through the University of Maine, taking two years off in the middle of his studies to earn enough money to finish, signing on with a logging crew in the foothills of western Maine, near his hometown. He had returned to graduate a year before I arrived on campus, and by the time we met he had already been working in Connecticut for a few years as a metallurgical engineer. If he could not exactly be called sophisticated, he did seem more grown-up than the other boys in many ways. That maturity, along with his easy, friendly manner, appealed to me, as I had, in the eleven years since my mother's death, grown into a rather shy and serious—some might have said far too serious—young woman.

Our friends introduced us. I liked him right away, and I could tell he liked me, too. Up to this point, however, his maturity hadn't extended to making sensible choices about girls. A month or so earlier, he'd met another girl at a party—the empty-headed sort of girl who bats her eyes and sways when she walks, and makes boys lose their heads. After knowing her for only a week or two, he had rather impulsively given her his fraternity pin. She was at that picnic too, flaunting the pin on the waistband of her shorts because—as my friends and I observed disapprovingly to each other while we watched her from across the lawn—there simply wasn't enough fabric in her skimpy halter top to pin it to.

After our initial introduction, I spent most of the day studiously ignoring Bill, flirting a little with some of his housemates and friends, letting him know with a toss of my head that I didn't have time to waste on a man who was otherwise involved. By the time night fell and we gathered around a bonfire on the shore, Bill had his Sigma Phi Sigma pin back. The girl had moved on, apparently with no hard feelings, to one of the several other boys who had been nudging each other all afternoon as they watched her out of the corners of their eyes. I don't even remember her name.

After that, Bill began calling for me two or three times a week at the YMCA, where, just as in my college dormitory, the house mother sat at a desk beside the front stairs and kept a sharp eye out to make sure no boys slipped by her to breach the girls' quarters. We strolled around the city in the warm summer evenings, sat on the benches in Elizabeth Park and talked and talked, and visited all the diners and coffee shops within walking distance, trying out their biscuits and meatloaf and pies—none of them, Bill insisted, quite as good as his grandmother's.

By Labor Day weekend, when I brought him to Bangor to introduce him to my father, Bill had bought a diamond ring and stashed the box in his pocket. I already knew full well by then that I was going to marry him, but when he produced the ring, I pretended to be shocked. Oh, no, I told him; it was far too soon—less than two months!—and I made him put it away to wait for our next visit to Bangor, at Christmas.

Once he'd spoken to my father, and put the diamond on my finger, Bill, who was already pushing thirty, said he didn't see any reason for a long engagement.

And so we were married in early April at the Hammond Street Congregational Church, with my best friend, Mac—she was another Ruth, really, Ruth McClelland, but no one ever called her anything but Mac—and Bill's college friend Harold as our attendants, and my brothers Shume and Don as ushers.

"April is the cruelest month," wrote T.S. Eliot, and in that year, 1942, April was particularly cruel to many young couples, as the United States' involvement in the war intensified. Husbands were sent overseas to fight, and wives did their best to keep up the home front.

But as for Bill and me, we couldn't imagine being any happier. Bill's age, his engineering background, and his work in metals testing meant that his own contribution to the war effort would be made from here at home. Soon after we returned from our honeymoon in New Hampshire, we spaded up a patch of ground in the backyard of our little square box of a house on Camp Avenue in Newington and planted a victory garden, growing our own tomatoes, carrots, beans, peas, beets, and lettuce. Each week, Bill had part of his paycheck withheld for the purchase of war bonds. We got used to driving at thirty-five miles per hour, and learned to cope with the rationing of sugar. We were proud to be doing our part.

June 17, 1958, Westfield, New Jersey

Ruth

I SUPPOSE I SHOULD FEEL BAD THAT THE four of them got up this morning—the morning after their father died—got themselves dressed, drank orange juice in the kitchen, and left for school. I suppose I should have stopped them, sent them back upstairs to change out of their school clothes. I should have called their schools and said—Greg's math test be damned—that my children were unable to attend today because their father had passed away.

It hadn't occurred to me that they would get up and go to school, but when I saw that that was what they intended, I didn't try to dissuade them. I had so much to do, and after today, the last day of the school year, there would be no structure of any kind for us to cling to, no outline to consult for the days that loomed ahead. Let them go, and keep to their routines as much as they could, for one more day.

Leslie slept with me last night, after crying herself into exhaustion on Bill's pillow. I'd changed the linens, of course, put the twisted, sweat-soaked sheets into the washing machine almost as soon as the men from the funeral home had left with his body. But, even so, Leslie pressed her face into the clean pillowcase and howled. "It smells like Da-a-a-ddy!" she wailed.

When she woke this morning, I had already been downstairs to start the coffee and help Grammy in the bathroom. I slipped back into the room, and she opened her swollen eyes. "Mommy, did I have a bad dream?" she whispered.

Now I watch her back as she trudges slowly down the sidewalk, trailing a little behind her brothers and scuffing the toes of her saddle shoes. What will the Sweets think when she appears at their kitchen door, as if this were any other school day, to walk to school with Diana? I turn away from the window and pour myself another cup of strong black coffee.

Winnie arrives at eight-thirty; it's been barely eight hours since she left. She is taking the next couple of days off from work, she says. I didn't want her to come, don't want her here now, but she tells me I need her, and of course she's right. Grammy can't be left alone for long, and I am due at the funeral home at ten to discuss the arrangements, which means choosing a casket, planning the service, and figuring out how to get Bill's body to Bethel.

Because of course that is where he will be buried, in the plot at Woodland Cemetery, next to his parents' graves. I think the train will be best, and certainly more economical than paying someone to drive a hearse all the way to Maine, although I hate the idea of his body being loaded and unloaded like ordinary freight.

I'll try not to think too much about it, and hope the kids won't ask any questions. I'll rely on the funeral home in New Jersey to communicate with the funeral home in Bethel and to leave me out of the specifics as much as possible.

By the time the kids and I get to Bethel at the end of the week, there Bill will be, as if he'd never left his home town, had lived out his life and died in Maine. That's what I know he would have wanted, after all, if only there had been a good living to be made there.

"Dad's plan for us"

Steve, Greg, Andy, Leslie

Greg: I did go to school the day after Dad died, and took my last final exam in seventh grade—math. (And aced it.)

Steve: Dad was to be a leader on a week-long camping trip to Blue Mountain Lake in the Adirondacks, where we were to help with the creation of Camp Sabattis on 1,300 acres of land that the Scout council had recently acquired.

When I went to school the next day, it was to practice for graduation from Roosevelt Junior High School at the end of my ninth grade year. I was asked during marching practice by a fellow Scout what time we would be leaving on the trip. I told him that I wasn't sure it was still on because my father had died the night before. He refused to believe me and said, "If your father died you wouldn't be at school now."

I was surprised by his reaction and told him that I *had* to be there; I was the graduation speaker! He didn't get it, as you don't. We were children of a very stoic mother.

We boys did all go to the Adirondacks. Tom Street served as Scoutmaster and was especially attentive to me. He had a tin of oatmeal raisin cookies in his car that his mother sent him with, and he and I would find excuses to go to the parking lot to sample them.

Leslie: I also remember going to school the next day and having complete strangers come up to me and ask if my father had died. I remember thinking, why don't they just make an all-school announcement over the loudspeaker, so people will stop asking me!

Andy: The night Dad died we kids sat up late with Mom. "What do we do now?" someone (me?) asked.

And Mom replied, "You'll do just what your father wanted you to do. You'll study hard, get good grades in school, earn scholarships, and go to college."

I didn't know that's what Dad had always wanted, but Mom said it so convincingly that it became the plan for our next decade or so.

Here's what I remember about the morning after Dad's death. Steve, Greg, and I were all sleeping in the attic. I awoke to Greg and Steve getting dressed. When I asked Greg what he was doing, he said, "Going to school."

Guess that was day one of Dad's plan for us.

1942–1955, Newington, Connecticut

Ruth

WHEN BILL GRADUATED FROM THE University of Maine in 1936, he stepped out of school into a world still mired in the Great Depression. Jobs for recent college graduates were scarce throughout the country, and nearly nonexistent in Maine. Connecticut—home of Sikorsky and Pratt & Whitney and the naval shipyards—was the logical place for a bright young engineer to go to seek his fortune.

By the time we met in 1941, with the country moving inexorably toward war, the opportunities there were only increasing. For the next few years, our tiny house in Newington was something of a way station for Bill's Bethel friends, who made their way to Connecticut to work and needed a place to stay until they found apartments of their own.

Bill had never meant to stay away forever. His sojourn in Connecticut was meant to provide him with a few years of experience, and perhaps a bit of a nest egg, that he could take back home with him. He knew he'd never earn the same kind of money back in Maine, but eventually, he hoped, opportunities for college-educated engineers might expand, even there. There might be work for him at the paper mill in Rumford, or at one of the other papermaking giants whose tall stacks belched smoke into the sky over towns like Millinocket, Bucksport, and Westbrook.

Then we met, and got married, and his focus quickly changed, from marking time to making a life.

But no matter that, as it turned out, Bill spent half his life outside of the state he always called home: he remained a Maine boy to the core. His weekend attire—plaid wool jacket and leather work boots—set him apart from the other suburban fathers in their windbreakers and smooth-soled loafers, and our boys were the only ones in the neighborhood who were allowed—even encouraged, though not so much by me—to build campfires, shoot a .22, and trap muskrats in the stream behind the Baxters' house across the street.

Everything was better in Maine, we told each other time and again, and we both knew it to be true. In Maine, the water was cold and clear, the people resourceful and clever. In the fall, the leaves were brighter. Sweet corn in the summer was sweeter. As we went about our days in suburban Connecticut, Maine had become our touchstone. We dreamed of getting back there—for vacations and, eventually, to live.

June 17, 1958, Westfield, New Jersey

Ruth

LAST NIGHT, AFTER WINNIE FINALLY LEFT, after I gave Grammy a sleeping pill, after Leslie sobbed herself to sleep, the boys and I sat at the kitchen table. I was drinking coffee; I had no plans to sleep. I'd told them once or twice to get ready for bed, but none of them had moved.

I looked at them and saw all at once that my children were leaving me. I saw the dark shadow on Steve's chin and upper lip and realized with a start that he must already have started to shave. I saw Greg draw himself up and grow inches taller, saw his shoulders grow wider as I watched. I saw the hint of cheekbones in Andy's round face, of hollows beneath his serious gray eyes.

Steve cleared his throat, and we all looked at him, waiting to see what he would say. "Well," he said, "I guess now we'll have to sell the camp."

The camp! It was the first time I had thought of it during the whole long, terrible evening. I felt something almost like relief wash over me at the realization that, after all, we had something of Bill to hold onto. We had something to work for together, something to sustain us, something to connect us to home—for, like Bill, I had never stopped thinking of Maine as "home."

But if Bill could really be gone, could the camp—our foundation, so central to how we saw ourselves as a family—still endure? He and the boys had built it together over the past three summers—Bill driving up every weekend to join us at the lake, the boys nearly bursting with excitement and pride at what they had accomplished while he'd been gone, eager for the next task he would set for them.

We had each poured the best of ourselves into the place, and had gotten back, in return, our even better selves. The kids, who seldom bickered anyway, went solid weeks without so much as raising their voices to each other when we were at camp. For my part, I felt myself become, at the lake, the wife and mother I had always intended to be—patient, spontaneous, unruffled. And Bill had always relaxed into his most genial and authentic self there—he slowed down, worried less, smoked less, joked more.

What would we find when we drove in the mile of rutted dirt road and came within sight of the cabin? Did the place still hold Bill's spirit? Was that the answer to the question I hadn't asked Reverend McCorison earlier that evening—where Bill was now? Or would we find the cabin bleak and lifeless, an empty shell, like the body that had been whisked away before the kids came home? Without him, were we still a family? Or were we a collection of separate souls—strangers sharing a lifeboat, or shaky survivors clinging to the rim of the same widening abyss?

The three of them were watching me, and I looked at them each in turn, pressing the palms of my hands flat against the tabletop to stop their shaking. I didn't know what my words would be until the moment I opened my mouth to say them.

"We are never going to sell the camp," I said simply. I didn't add, "I promise" or "you have my word on it," but they heard the authority in my voice, and they nodded. Their shoulders slumped just a little, letting go of a fraction of the tension that had kept them rigid.

With my words, I made the leap of faith that allowed me to keep believing in the dream Bill and I had shared: long, languorous summers of freedom at the lake, the restorative powers of our time in Maine. Because, it was suddenly clear to me, we, as survivors, needed that time, that place, more now than ever. We would call upon it to heal so much more now than the strain of our busy suburban life, the life that none of us—Bill least of all—had ever felt was a proper fit.

1942–1955, Newington, Connecticut

Ruth

In May of 1942, just a month after we were married, Connecticut, like the other eastern states, instituted gasoline rationing, and suddenly we found that we were unable to take the trip to Maine we had planned for that summer. As happy as I was in my new state of domestic bliss, it gave me a peculiar, unsettled feeling to realize that we were, at least for now, effectively exiled from home.

Back in Maine, my brother Don was graduating from Bangor High School, making plans to start at the University in the fall, and getting ever more serious with his girl, Leota. In Bethel, Bill's grandmother had just turned eighty-one, but she and his mother soldiered on at their restaurant, up before dawn to start the baking. They were alone by then, except for Ruby, the hired girl. Bill's younger sister, Kaye, had left for Connecticut after her graduation from Gould Academy three years earlier. She'd received her R.N. from Hartford Hospital, and now she was serving in the Navy Nurse Corps.

I knew I'd never go back to Bangor to live. Too many somber memories haunted my father's square yellow house on Boutelle Road, where my brothers and I had done our best to raise ourselves after our mother's death. A visit there once or twice a year was all I needed to remind me of why I'd left.

But I still felt drawn to my home state, unwilling to give up my identity as a hardy Maine girl, and not above playing it up a bit around some of the more delicate Connecticut girls I met. No one needed to know that my hometown was really what passed for a big city in Maine, that the trolley had run nearly within sight of my house, or that I'd grown up hearing planes take off and land at nearby Godfrey Field.

Instead, I easily adopted Bill's Maine, where strong, stoic women donned plaid woolen shirts to do barn chores, or stoked the woodstove in a logging camp to bake biscuits for a hundred hungry men. These were the legendary women of the western Maine foothills that he called home, and I aspired to be every bit as hardy and robust.

Like me, Bill, too, had lost a parent—his father—at a young age, and his family's life in Bethel from then on must, in many ways, have been harsh. His father and grandfather had both died in 1924, the year he turned twelve. His grandparents, William and Addie Farwell, had left the farm on a hill east of town where they'd raised their large family to move into the village only the year before. They'd bought a small building on Church Street and converted it into a store and tea room. When first Bill's father, then his grandfather, died unexpectedly in March, just nine days apart, the two widows joined forces to run the tea room together as Farwell & Wight's, expanding the menu to include full meals as well as an array of breads, pastries, cookies, and cakes.

The women worked from before dawn until late in the day, and Bill was expected to help out in any way he could, chopping and hauling wood for the stoves in the restaurant and their apartment upstairs, fetching ice, running errands, washing dishes during the busiest times, and minding Kaye, who was not quite three when their father died. From the sound of it, whenever he wasn't in school, he was working, and there couldn't have been much time left over for fun.

Yet the stories he told were full of his outdoor adventures, of hours spent roaming the wooded trails, often with Kaye on his shoulders. He hiked the mountains and fished the brooks, hunted for arrowheads and dug for minerals, and played practical jokes with his friends. Somehow he managed to make the most of what little freedom he was allowed.

Bill had been in Connecticut for five years by the time we met, but he told me, right from the day of that picnic at Hitchcock Lake, that his heart was set on moving back to his hometown one day. It quickly became our shared dream, central to all the plans we made together for our future. "When we move home to Maine," we said, and with our words we painted for each other a picture of the life we'd live, of the house we'd build on a hill just outside of town, with the woods in our backyard and the mountains beyond our front windows.

After we married, we stayed on in Connecticut, thinking, at first, that we might find our way back to Maine within a few years. But we settled in and made friends. We got a dog, and pretty soon we started having babies. Steve arrived in the fall of 1943, and Greg two years later. By the time Andy was born, on the last day of 1946, we were outgrowing our tiny house on Camp Avenue in Newington, and eventually we moved to a bigger one, our wonderful home on Main Street. When our best friends, Betty and Elmer Baxter, exiled Mainers like us, bought the house right across the street, our suburban life seemed to us almost perfect, at least for the time being.

After three boys, finally, our fourth baby was a girl—although we chose to name her Leslie, after Bill's uncle, and Bill taught her all he could about the outdoors, just as he did the boys. On summer weekends, we packed up the family and went on camping trips to what remained of the Connecticut wilderness. The kids learned how to use an axe and a pocketknife, how to identify poison ivy, and how to build a campfire. I learned to patch up minor cuts, scrapes, bites, and burns, when to call our family doctor for advice, and when to head for the emergency room.

Most years, we spent Bill's longer summer vacation in Maine. I was losing touch with many of my friends from high school and college, most of whom had married and moved away, and although we divided our time, when in Maine, between our respective parents, our dutiful visits to my father's somber home in Bangor were brief. By then, my heart belonged to the western Maine mountains and lakes, and the busy little town of Bethel. Despite the miles that separated him from his hometown, Bill had always made it a priority to maintain his close connection to the people and events there, and when he returned he was always welcomed as a native son.

"I was raised in Connecticut, but I grew up in Maine"

Steve, Greg, Andy, Leslie

Andy: We grew up feeling Maine was our real homeland, and our life in Connecticut and New Jersey was temporary displacement. I hated the move to New Jersey because it was farther from Maine. I know it was economic necessity for Dad to go there for work, but for years I irrationally blamed New Jersey for his early death.

Greg: From Newington, we traveled several summers to Ada Balentine's camp on North Pond for two weeks. I remember motor boating up the lake to see the lot with the big rock before we bought it.

One strong memory, I suppose from one of the years we vacationed in Ada's camp, was arriving in Bethel at Pete Chapin's Shell station, sitting in the car and listening to Dad and Pete josh each other. Never before or after did I hear Dad cuss, but then he did, at least twice. It was like he was recalling his wilder teen years with unfettered joy.

Earlier, before the camp lot in Maine, we had a lot in Simsbury, where Dad chopped his arm.

Andy: I have to laugh about our family lore of Dad the woodsman whacking himself with an axe. And especially the part about Mom not knowing how to drive, jamming their car in some gear and driving him, hell bent for leather, to get emergency care.

Steve: Dad cut his arm trimming branches off some trees that he had cleared from the lot in Simsbury, where he planned to build a camp three roads back from the lake. Mom did transport him to the hospital, minus a license. He was assigned a bed in the so-called "alcoholic ward" and, thanks to his inebriated roommate, that was how the quote "Charlie wants some ice in his milk" became a household saying!

Leslie: One of my favorite memories of Dad and Maine was going with him to Bumpus mine in Albany to collect rocks. We'd come home with sacks full of rose quartz, smoky quartz, feldspar, and an occasional piece of tourmaline or beryl. I remember my excitement one time when we found lavender lepidolite! I'm not sure which I loved more, the stone or its name. I just loved how the words felt as they rolled off my tongue—lavender lepidolite. I repeated them over and over again.

Andy: The fact that we spent literally the whole summer at the lake year after year meant the bulk of our "free" time was Maine-based and we did not build bonds with friends and classmates in suburbia. A loss in many ways, but it further strengthened our family bonds.

When asked where I am from, I always say I was raised in Connecticut, but I grew up in Maine.

June 17, 1958, Westfield, New Jersey

Ruth

BEFORE IT IS TIME TO LEAVE FOR THE funeral home, I sit at the dining room table with a pen and a pad of lined paper to write Bill's obituary. The window behind me is open to let in the cool morning air, and a bird in the maple tree is singing the same two notes, over and over. In the kitchen, I hear Winnie speaking to Grammy in the low, soothing tones one might use with a child. I glance into the living room, at the mantel clock above the fireplace. Nearly nine o'clock. Bill has been dead for thirteen hours.

There is a box of photographs in the middle of the table, a jumble of snapshots from the past sixteen years. I've already pulled out a three by five print of the only recent professional portrait of Bill, taken a year or so ago. It's a good likeness; a faint smile deepens the lines, like parentheses, that bracket his mouth, and his eyes glint from their deep sockets with barely restrained merriment. He wears a ridiculous tie with large, garish flowers. There is a deeper crease in his forehead above the inner corner of his left

eye than above his right, and the shape of his left ear is so dear
and familiar that suddenly, as I reach out a finger to trace it softly,
I can't remember how to inhale.

Neither the *Hartford Courant* nor the weekly *Westfield Leader*
will run a photograph with the obituary, but the *Bethel Citizen*, in
his hometown, might, especially since Bill still has family there. I
won't have time to do more than scribble out a handwritten copy
this morning before I go to the funeral home, where a secretary
will type it up and see that it is sent to the *Leader* and the *Courant*,
but I've slid a piece of carbon paper under the top sheet in the
pad. Later, when I have a few minutes, I'll get out my typewriter,
type up a neat copy, and place it in an envelope with the photograph. I'll drop it off at the *Citizen* office on Friday before the burial, in plenty of time to appear in next week's edition of the paper.

At the top of the box of photographs is a creased snapshot of
Bill and the kids, seated in a row on boulders on the summit of
Cadillac Mountain in Acadia National Park. I took it on a vacation
six years ago. We'd camped nearby, awoken the kids before day-
light, and driven up the auto road to catch the sunrise. Behind
them, the islands of Frenchman's Bay, with their spiky spruces,
look like half-submerged porcupines. Bill wears a dark shirt and a
tie—I don't remember why—his sleeves rolled up to the elbow. The
boys are in matching V-neck sweaters I knit for them, each with
the silhouette of a cowboy riding a bucking bronco on the front.
Andy leans on Bill's knee.

Beneath it are other photographs, so many of them taken in Maine. Bill and me, returning from our honeymoon to my father's house in Bangor, unloading from the car the spool bed frame we'd snowshoed up a mountain to retrieve from his grandparents' abandoned farmhouse in East Bethel. The bed we brought with us to Camp Avenue in Newington, to Main Street, and here, to Fairfield Circle in Westfield. The bed we still sleep in. No, the bed *I* still sleep in. The bed where Bill died.

A wide print of a 1954 family reunion photo, my side—my father in the center, his four grown children and their spouses beside him, our children arrayed on the grass at our feet, the ocean behind us. It was the last time my brother Shume was home in Maine, and the first time he had brought his children from California, where he was stationed, to meet their grandfather. After so many years of estrangement, I'd hoped my father's heart would soften when he held their babies and saw that, despite his reservations when Shume and Jerry married, they had made a good life together. But whatever had passed between them ten years before, whatever it was that had made Shume slam the back door as he left, spinning his tires and tossing the tidy white stones my father spread on his driveway onto his precious lawn, was still hanging there in the air. You could see it at the reunion picnic that day at the coast, in the way my father refused to meet Shume's eyes when they both reached for the same paper cup of lemonade, in the way he was cordial as Jerry passed him the potato salad, but no more than that.

"William Walton Wight, 45, of 652 Fairfield Circle, died suddenly Monday," I write, as if describing an event that happened to a stranger. "He was the husband of Ruth W. Wight."

What next? I look at the obituaries in a copy of last week's *Westfield Leader* and see that, for men, career and military service usually follow the details of the death and the mention of the widow.

Bill, of course, had no military service to list. Not that he hadn't tried his hardest to enlist during the war, no matter what I had to say about it. He was thirty years old, newly married, with a baby on the way, but still he presented himself, not once, but three times, at the recruiting office and said he was ready to go and fight.

The first time, he never even told me what he'd done until after he'd gotten a letter in the mail, thanking him for his patriotism and explaining that at present the ranks were being kept adequately full, by way of the draft and voluntary enlistment, with eighteen- to twenty-five-year-olds, but they would certainly notify him if they were in need of his service.

I pitched a fit, told him he had too many responsibilities, and was too old in any case, but that didn't stop him from trying twice more. In June of 1944, when he was about to turn thirty-two, and Steve was eight months old, Bill received a detailed letter explaining that his value to the war effort was greater in his capacity as a materials engineer, working stateside, than as a soldier, and that seemed, finally, to satisfy him.

"Mr. Wight was employed as a quality control supervisor for the New Jersey Division of the Kelsey-Hayes Company of Clark. He joined the firm three years ago after working for nineteen years as a metallurgist for Pratt & Whitney Small Tool Company of West Hartford, Connecticut," I write, thinking how impossible it seems that three years have gone by since we left Newington. Westfield still feels new to me, and our friends here, all but the Sweets, are the kind one makes through the convenience of proximity, rather than a meeting of minds.

I read over the two paragraphs, noticing that my handwriting is shaky, the result, no doubt, of sleeplessness, three or four cups of black coffee, and no breakfast. When I first sat down in the dining room with my pad of paper and pen, Winnie bustled in from the kitchen to set a plate of buttered toast on the table in front of me, but I have reached only for the coffee cup beside it. The toast is cold now, the butter—margarine, really—congealed on its surface, oily and yellow. Just looking at it makes my stomach lurch, and smelling it is worse. I push the plate to the far side of the table, and place the box of photographs so as to hide it from view.

Nothing I have written so far says anything about who Bill really was. I wish I could have started off, instead, like this: "Bill Wight, a good Maine boy, exiled to New Jersey, died tragically young, before he had a chance to return home. He loved his wife, his children, and his mother. He was clever, kind, generous, and honorable. Because he was raised in Maine, he could do anything,

build anything, fix anything. He liked apple pie with sharp ched-
dar cheese for breakfast, peanut butter and sardine sandwiches,
and baked beans on Saturday night."

But the paper wouldn't print anything like that, and I have only
two hundred words to try to sum up his life. In order to make his
Maine roots known, I have to settle for writing that he was born
in Oquossoc, and that he graduated from the University of Maine.
At the very end, after a mention of the funeral service, which will
be over by the time the paper comes out on Thursday, I write, "Burial will be in the Woodland Cemetery, Bethel, Maine."

Interspersed with those references to Maine, I include that Bill
was a member of the First Congregational Church in Westfield,
the American Society for Metals (and past chairman of its
Hartford chapter), and Sequin Lodge, A.F. & A.M. of Newington,
Connecticut. I add, as well, "Mr. Wight was active in Boy Scout
work here," bits of information that, I hope, will tell more about
the man he was than the dates of his birth and death and what he
did for work.

I list the survivors, "besides his widow": the boys in order of
age, Leslie, Grammy, and Kaye, then I carefully count the words to
see if I will have to leave anything out. It comes to exactly two
hundred and three, so I change "He was graduated from the University of Maine with the class of 1936" to "He was graduated from
the University of Maine in 1936," saving three words.

I tear off the top sheet, leaving the carbon copy on the pad, fold
it once, and put it into the outside pocket of my purse. I walk
briskly through the kitchen to the side door, letting Winnie and
Grammy know I'm leaving.

1953–1954, Woodstock, Maine

Ruth

IN THE SUMMER OF 1953, WE rented a camp on North Pond, a few miles south of Bethel in Woodstock. It belonged to my mother-in-law's friend Ada Balentine, a widow who stayed there herself for most of the summer, but who was happy to rent it out for a couple of weeks to help pay her taxes. It was a log cabin, set off by itself at the north end of the pond, far from the main road. At night, it was so quiet that we could hear dairy cows snuffling and blowing in their barn on the Gore Road, along the western shore. After the kids were asleep, Bill and I sat on the screened porch and looked over at the dark east side of the lake, where no road had yet been built, and imagined the lights of our own cabin shining out over the water.

We rented Ada's cabin again the next summer, and by that time lots were being offered for sale along the undeveloped eastern shore of North Pond. On a bright, warm afternoon, without telling them where we were going, we took the kids, in Ada's wooden motorboat, to a spot halfway down the lake, and brought the boat to shore beside a flat-topped boulder the size of a pickup truck that lay just touching land at the edge of the water. The boys hopped easily back and forth from the shore to the top of the big rock, then helped four-year-old Leslie across.

"It's a sunny rock," she announced with great satisfaction, plopping down to sit on the warm granite.

Bill looked at me, and I nodded. "This is the one we want," I said quietly. "The one with Sunny Rock."

Steve and Andy, clambering over the thick brush along the shore a few yards away, didn't hear my words, but Greg paused, one foot on the shore and one on the rock. He looked from his father to me.

"What do you mean?"

"This is the lot where we want to build our camp." Bill said this off-handedly, in the same tone he might have used to talk about the weather. He winked at me.

"But not really, right? You mean, if we really *could* build a camp." A dark flush spread over Greg's neck and face, turning the tips of his ears bright red. "Right?"

"Oh, let's do it!" Bill said, as if just now making up his mind. As if we hadn't been talking about it for a year—evenings after the kids were asleep, and mornings before we got out of bed, when the half-light of dawn woke us early. As if we hadn't gone over and over our finances, working out how we could spare the two-hundred-dollar asking price for the lot, then a few hundred more to purchase the materials we'd need to build a simple cabin.

"Come here, kids," Bill called to them. "Your mother and I want to tell you something."

June 17, 1958, Westfield, New Jersey

Ruth

AT THE FUNERAL HOME, I SLIDE THE folded sheet of lined paper across the wide desk to Mr. Gray. He begins to scan it, his lips moving as he reads, and almost immediately he looks up.

"You won't want to say 'died suddenly,'" he says, his voice firm.

What would I call Bill's death, if not sudden? I open my mouth to say this, but he is shaking his head.

"People read 'died suddenly' in the newspaper, and they think right away of a suicide. I'm sorry to have to say that to you, Mrs. Wight, but that's the way it is. You'll want to say 'died after a brief illness' instead."

"I can't say that," I protest. "He was on a business trip to the city the same day he died. People saw him in church on Sunday, at work yesterday. They all know he wasn't ill."

Mr. Gray shakes his head, says nothing, waits.

"Well, then, just say he died of a heart attack. That will make it plain enough."

I can tell that Mr. Gray doesn't like this much better. It's too blunt; it says more than he would like to tell people. It has a harsh, medical ring to it. But he acquiesces, and, with a sigh, crosses out the word "suddenly" and crowds "of a heart attack" in the space above it. I hope the newspapers won't quibble about the three extra words.

As for the funeral arrangements, I tell him, the service will be tomorrow. Again, Mr. Gray balks—he reminds me, in a soft voice that betrays none of the urgency he is probably feeling, that friends and relatives from out of town will need time to make their travel arrangements, that tomorrow is *very* soon, that perhaps Thursday would be better—but I am firm. Having thought it over throughout the night, I've realized that if the boys are to leave on Sunday for their Scout trip to the Adirondacks—which of course they must do; it's been planned for months—we'll need to schedule carefully and not waste any time.

So, the funeral is planned for eight o'clock on Wednesday evening. I would have preferred it to be earlier, but Mr. Gray already has a funeral scheduled for the morning and another for the afternoon, he tells me, a bit defensively, as if he expects me to insist that he rearrange the schedule.

Then the casket I will choose—the simplest one they show me, which is still too ornate and expensive—with Bill's body inside, resting, in his best suit, on the padded ivory lining, will make the trip to Bethel by train for the committal service on Saturday morning. We'll drive the eight hours to Maine on Friday, and back to Westfield on Saturday after the burial. It will all work; all of the necessary events will fit into the time we have available, and I feel a flicker of pride in my organizational skills.

I know that Bill would have been happier with a box of rough pine boards, knocked together with nails, like the one in which his father was no doubt laid to rest after his own sudden death. But of course they don't offer me anything like that.

I know what Mr. Gray would think if I asked about a plain pine coffin, even though he wouldn't say it: This isn't the frontier, ma'am; this isn't the nineteenth century. This is 1958, and Gray's is an up-to-date funeral home. All of our caskets are made to modern standards and the latest designs.

He begins to describe the merits of double walls and moisture barriers, how much things have changed for the better in the industry, so that caskets now offer "greatly improved protection." Protection from what? I wonder. I assume—even though it's mid-June in New Jersey, oppressively hot and humid—that whatever they've done with fluids and chemicals to prepare Bill's body for the funeral will get us through the service at the cemetery in Bethel on Saturday. Just how long does a body need to remain intact once it's in the ground? I barely listen as Mr. Gray points out the unique features of each casket.

In the end, I don't believe it matters much. Whatever it was that made Bill who he was—call it his soul or his spirit or his essence—has nearly as little to do with his body as it does with the empty suits and shirts hanging in our bedroom closet. The sort of box I choose to put it in, that body he no longer inhabits, is of so little importance, really, that I may as well economize.

Standing in the center of a large room, its walls lined with double tiers of caskets of every price and quality, I hear Bill speaking to me for the first time since his death. Although "hear" isn't exactly right, because I don't turn around, stunned, to see where the voice is coming from. I don't look sharply at Mr. Gray and his assistant to see if they've heard it, too. I know perfectly well that I am the only one Bill is addressing when he says, "You may as well economize, Ruth."

You're right, I think. We can put the money I'll save toward finishing the camp. I know this would please him, although it doesn't seem to please Mr. Gray.

While it is, of course, my decision, Mr. Gray tells me, he feels obliged, he says, to point out that while the outer materials of *all* of their caskets are of fine quality, and they all have a quilted satin lining that *appears* similar, between the layers of the cheaper models is—his voice drops lower—an inner core of paperboard. Furthermore—his voice drops again, so that I have to lean closer to hear him—the satin in this particular model is stapled, not sewn, in place.

"But I don't want an open casket at the service," I remind him; we've already been over this decision. "No one will even see it."

He shakes his head almost imperceptibly and repeats that of course it is up to me, and I summon up the brisk tone I use to get Leslie to finish her peas, or the bridge club to stop gossiping and play cards.

"This will be fine," I say.

Mr. Gray's sigh is only barely audible.

When I get back from the funeral home, my sister-in-law Leota's car is parked next to Winnie's in the driveway. She's picked up Betty in Newington and driven down for Steve's junior high graduation. After I was finally able to shoo Reverend McCorison out the door last night—I managed to be civil to him, though I was furious after how I'd heard him break the news to the boys—my first call was to my brother Don. Shocked, he'd broken down on the phone, wanted to get in the car right then and drive the three hours to be with me, but as much as I longed to see him, I said no.

"Come tomorrow, if you can. If you want to. It's Steve's graduation tomorrow evening."

"Oh, Ruth, you can't be thinking you'll go to that!" It was Leota's voice, through sobs, on their bedroom extension.

Don agreed. "No one will expect you to be there, not now, Ruthie."

"Steve's making a speech."

"He doesn't have to do that, Ruthie. Have you asked him if he still wants to do it?"

But I didn't need to ask Steve, of course. Like me, my children would do what had to be done.

August 27, 1954, Woodstock, Maine

Ruth

THE DATE THAT WAS SET FOR THE closing on our purchase of the lot was a Friday at the end of August. We'd only been back in Connecticut after our vacation on the lake for two weeks, and Bill didn't feel he could take any more time off from work just then, so it was decided that I would be the one to drive up that morning to the law office in South Paris where the transaction would take place, taking Leslie along for company. We would spend the night in Bethel, with Grammy, and return home on Saturday.

It would be the first time I had ever driven from Connecticut to Maine by myself, without Bill. I was nervous the night before, which made me irritable and snappish. Then Bill turned on the radio to catch the news and we learned that a tropical depression had formed over the Bahamas and was heading north, picking up speed off the Florida coast. It had a name now, Carol, and some meteorologists thought it was likely to attain full hurricane status over the next couple of days.

"Don't worry about that," Bill assured me. "It probably won't come anywhere near us."

"You don't know that."

"Even if it does, you'll be back home before it ever makes it this far up the coast."

"You don't know that, either!" I had visions of huddling in the station wagon along some godforsaken stretch of Route 26 while Leslie howled in terror as trees were uprooted and limbs crashed onto the car.

Once we were on the road, though, just after sunrise, I relaxed. The drive up was uneventful, and we arrived in South Paris in time to stop beside the fountain in Moore Park and eat the sandwiches I'd packed for us before we drove to the lawyer's office. It was chilly, and Leslie shivered in her shorts and t-shirt. I checked my purse, for perhaps the tenth time, and found the check still tucked securely into an inside pocket. One hundred and eighty dollars—

the asking price of the lot, less the twenty dollars Bill had pulled from his wallet and handed to Earle Palmer the day after we'd shown it to the kids for the first time.

An hour later, the papers were signed, and—according to the formal language of the deed—"a certain lot or parcel of land situated in Woodstock, in said County of Oxford and State of Maine" was ours. At last, we held the title to our own piece of Maine—"Lot #10, in Mann Camp Lots Hamlin Grant #13," to be specific.

Hamlin Grant, more properly called Hamlin's Gore, was the result of an early nineteenth century surveyor's error. Originally intended as part of a land grant to Dummer Academy, which became the western part of the township of Woodstock, the long narrow strip of land called Hamlin's Gore was accidentally left off of the survey, becoming a sort of no man's land between the Dummer Academy Grant and Bethel. For nearly sixty years, until it was annexed to the town of Woodstock, Hamlin's Gore existed as an independent plantation, with a schoolhouse and roads, and its own government of elected officers.

Bill had read us the whole story from a worn copy of William B. Lapham's 1882 *History of Woodstock, Maine*, which he had found on a rainy-day visit to the Bethel Library during our vacation. The staunchly temperate town of Woodstock had finally annexed Hamlin's Gore in 1873—expressly to put an end to a thriving liquor business being run out of a brick house belonging to a bold miscreant by the name of John Merrill, at the corner of the Gore Road and what is now Route 232. Merrill had ensured the continuation of his liquor license from year to year by serving as a member of the plantation's licensing board. After being put out of business, he departed Hamlin's Gore for parts unknown, leaving a large sum owing to his supplier, the state liquor agent, which eventually had to be paid by his former neighbors. Bill laughed out loud, right there in the library, when he read this bit of information; he loved learning that our camp lot lay just up the road from the former home of a local scofflaw.

"Look, our lot is in Hamlin Grant number thirteen." I pointed out the words on the deed to Leslie. "Thirteen is my lucky number."

I wasn't superstitious, of course. I didn't believe it was bad luck to spill salt or break a mirror or open an umbrella in the house. I didn't believe in good luck, either—in crossed fingers or rabbit's feet or four-leaf clovers. But I was born on the thirteenth day of February in 1920, a Friday, and I had once heard my mother assert—in response to a neighbor who had suggested that I would be unlucky all my life as a result of such an unfortunate birthdate—that thirteen was a lucky number for anyone born on that day of the month. I didn't really believe that, even as a child, but it gave me a reason to be proud of the date of my birth, rather than try to hide it.

I hadn't planned to visit the lot on this quick trip, but when we passed the roadside spring on our way to Lena's house and drew near the right turn off of the main road that led to it, I found I couldn't go past without stopping.

"We'll just go and have a quick look."

The dirt road was narrow and rutted, more loam and clay than gravel, with protruding roots and rocks, and standing puddles from the last rainstorm. Leafy branches scraped the windows as I navigated the car slowly between the ditches and tried not to let it bottom out. It was a mile in the road to the lot, but it felt like ten, and I prayed I wouldn't meet another car and have to back up.

There were six camps on the east shore already. Two had been built around 1950, before the road was put in—one on the former site of a cabin called Camp Comfort that had stood, tucked into a cove on the wild shore, since the 1890s; the other further north along the shore—by floating the lumber across the lake. The second of these camps, two tenths of a mile or so beyond our lot, belonged to Stan Andrews, who had rafted the lumber to build his camp across the lake on an old barn door. Stan's wife, Gertrude, was a daughter of Edwin Mann, whose logging company had purchased the land along the eastern shore, harvested most of the marketable timber, then divided it up for sale as camp lots. Stan owned the hardware store in Bryant Pond village, and he and Gertrude had three little girls.

Another of Mr. Mann's sons-in-law, Earle Palmer, who had handled the transaction when we purchased our lot, had just gotten the frame of his camp up, roofed, and closed in that summer. His lot was a small island just off a marshy section of the shore, and he'd connected it to the mainland with a corduroy causeway across the marsh. The causeway was built from load after load of birch edgings from the Mann Company's clothespin mill, which he'd dumped into the lake, weighting them down and filling around them with loads of stony gravel so they wouldn't float away when the water rose after a hard rain.

The Hathaways had built their camp, invisible to Leslie and me as we drove by, on a large lot at the end of a long driveway that led to a secluded cove. Many years later, two of their children would add camps of their own to the same sandy stretch of shoreline, forming a private family compound.

The other two camps, Bickfords' and Baldwins', were brand new, built side by side on shallow lots at a spot where the road came close to the shore and the ground rose steeply on the uphill side of it. There were two empty lots between the Baldwins' camp and our newly-acquired property, For Sale signs tacked to a tree on each.

There was no place yet on our lot to pull off the road, and the only place to turn around was a quarter-mile further on, where the road dead-ended in a spot just wide enough to back around. This I did, then left the car in the road beside our lot while Leslie and I picked our way through the thick brush to the edge of the pond.

I had hoped that we might sit together on the shore, atop the big boulder Leslie had named Sunny Rock, and enjoy the afternoon sunshine, but the weather was breezy and felt like fall. We wrapped our arms around ourselves to stay warm and stood looking out at the lake, where the wind kicked up whitecaps that sparkled in the sun.

June 17, 1958, Westfield, New Jersey

Ruth

EVERYONE IS CRYING WHEN I WALK INTO the kitchen—Leota and Betty, Winnie, Grammy in her chair by the window, and our neighbor Marge, who turns from the open refrigerator where she has been trying to find a spot for something in a covered dish—everyone but me.

When Betty hugs me I cling to her and feel her ample chest heaving with sobs. Leota, although she's as perfectly put-together as always—never without makeup, hair always in place—clutches a pale blue handkerchief, edged with lace and stained with mascara, and dabs at her eyes.

I look around for Don, but Leota, seeing my gaze go around the room, shakes her head.

"He couldn't come today, Ruth. He has to pick your father up at the airport this afternoon. They'll be here tomorrow morning. My mother is flying down with Dad so she can take care of the kids for us tomorrow when we come back for the—for Bill's—"

She breaks off, unable to go on, and presses the sodden handkerchief to her mouth.

These two women, the dearest in my world, have each left three children at home and driven well over a hundred miles to be here with me, and my knees are weak with a rush of gratitude. There is a lump in my throat like the stone of a peach, and I touch my cheek, expecting to find tears there, but still, none come.

The kids will be home soon—they are being dismissed early on this last day of the school year, at one o'clock instead of three. Leota pulls out a chair at the kitchen table and makes me sit down. From the refrigerator she pulls deli meats, sliced cheeses, pickles, olives—extravagant things I never buy, the bounty that comes along with a tragedy. She begins to make sandwiches, cutting them into triangles, piling them on a platter. The teakettle whistles, and she sets a mug in front of me—just weak tea, without sugar or lemon or milk, exactly the way I like it. I take the first sip, and realize it's Constant Comment, the fancy blend with orange rind and sweet spices that Bill and the kids buy me every year for my birthday. I save it for special occasions—which, I suppose, this is.

By the time the kids get home, Leota has run a load of wash and hung it to dry on the lines in the backyard; when she opens the door to the basement I can hear a second load sloshing in the machine. She has pulled everything out of the refrigerator, labeled each covered dish, organized and stacked them, and decided which of the half-dozen casseroles—delivered by various neighbors this morning while I was out—we'll have for supper. She has washed the dishes, swept the kitchen floor, helped Grammy to and from the bathroom. She's a bundle of nervous energy and knows how to put it to good use.

I am still sitting in the same spot at the table. I've switched from tea to black coffee, and the cooling dregs of my second—third?—cup of the afternoon are in front of me, a triangle of ham sandwich, the edges of the bread growing dry, on the saucer. Betty is beside me, her right hand covering my left where it rests on the table, not talking, just being there.

1955, Newington, Connecticut

Ruth

FOR CHRISTMAS IN 1954, THE YEAR we bought the lot, Bill gave each of the boys a hammer of his own. I made nail aprons from heavy denim, including a tiny one for Leslie, who was five. The biggest, heaviest gift under the tree was addressed "To Ruth, From Santa." I tore away the brown wrapping paper to find a wooden keg of eight-penny nails, a hundred pounds of them.

A couple of days after Christmas, when our husbands had gone back to their jobs, a group of women from the neighborhood met for coffee at Betty's house across the street, as we often did. We compared notes on the holiday.

"Elmer gave me books," Betty said happily. "The Chronicles of Narnia to read to the boys, and the new one by Anya Seton for me."

"I got an electric sewing machine—finally," said Jean, who loved to sew. For years she had managed to turn out beautiful clothing for her family on an old treadle machine that had been her grand-mother's.

"Earrings and a necklace." We all sighed when Barbara said this—imagine getting jewelry from our husbands! "Now I just have to get Fred to take me somewhere so I can wear them." We laughed.

"I got a keg of nails." I pretended to sound rueful.

"What!" they all cried.

"To build our camp in Maine," I added, smiling.

We planned and dreamed all that winter. I sketched floor plans on the backs of old envelopes and the kids' school papers, and showed them to Bill in the evenings when he got home from work. He took most of my suggestions and drew up a set of workable plans, covered with measurements and notes in the small, neat handwriting of an engineer. We began to make lists of the materials we'd need and to figure out how much they would cost.

I let down the hems of Leslie's school dresses, patched the knees of the boys' pants, scrimped at the grocery store, and put every bit of money I could save into an old coffee can in the spice cupboard. At the end of each month, we counted the money in the can and put it in a manila envelope Bill kept in his desk, adding the figure to the outside. In February, when my father sent money for my birthday, it went right into the envelope.

"Are you sure?" Bill asked, knowing that I could have used a new dress, that the wallpaper in our bedroom was faded and out-dated, that my electric mixer overheated every time I ran it for more than a minute. But I nodded; I was sure.

Then, in the spring, when we were making plans to spend the summer on the lake—the kids and I would stay for two whole months, and Bill would join us on weekends, and for a three-week vacation in August—came the offer of a new job, in New Jersey.

Bill hadn't had a raise in three years at Pratt & Whitney Machine Tool Company, where he had worked ever since coming down to Connecticut from Maine after his college graduation in 1936. Pratt & Whitney Machine Tool was a relatively small company, making precision instruments in West Hartford. Except for sharing a name, it had never really had much to do with the manufacturing giant, Pratt & Whitney Aircraft. That was where the really good jobs were, and where my brother Don had gone to work once he'd returned from his stint in the army and finished college.

I always felt compelled to explain this difference to new ac-quaintances; I could see them jump to conclusions about our eco-nomic status when they heard where Bill worked, and that he was an engineer. Pratt & Whitney Aircraft, started by Frederick Rentschler in the mid-1920s in an unused part of Pratt & Whitney Machine Tool's facility (and with a quarter-million-dollar loan from the company), had grown by leaps and bounds, of course, especially during the war. Rentschler had long since outgrown the little corner of the tool plant where he'd started out and ended his association with Pratt & Whitney Machine Tool. By the close of the 1920s, he had merged his company with Boeing and other big names in aviation, and relocated to a vast new headquarters in East Hartford.

Even if it wasn't on a par with the huge aircraft manufacturer, Pratt & Whitney Machine Tool was still a good company in many ways. Bill was well respected there, and after nineteen years he felt the pull of loyalty toward his coworkers and supervisors. His direct boss, Ernie Bancroft, better known to everyone as "Whiff," never failed to show his appreciation for Bill's skills, intelligence, and work ethic.

But all of that did nothing to change the fact that he had four kids to support now, and with the dizzying growth of the war years long over, it didn't look like he'd be getting much of a raise any time soon.

I cried when the offer came. Although I'd agreed with Bill that his prospects for advancement with Pratt & Whitney Machine Tool seemed stagnant, that he wasn't being paid what he was worth, that it was time to put out feelers elsewhere, I hadn't ever meant for him to look outside of the Hartford area. All of us loved our big old house on Main Street in Newington, where we'd moved eight years earlier—loved the neighborhood, loved running back and forth to Elmer and Betty's across the street, and the Schicks' house next door.

When he'd sent his resume to Cooper Alloy in Clark, New Jersey, I had prayed it would be lost in the mail. When he was called to the company's headquarters for an interview, I prayed our old station wagon would break down on the turnpike. When he returned home and said he thought it had gone well, I prayed that he was wrong. When they made him a salary offer, I prayed it would be lower than he'd expected.

I knew what my role was, of course. It was my job to smile, to congratulate Bill, to tell him I was sure it was all for the best, how wonderful it was that he would—finally—get the salary he deserved. It was my job to tell the kids, convincingly, what an exciting adventure this would be for all of us, how lucky we were that we'd all get to make new friends—though we'd still keep the old ones, of course, and we'd visit Newington whenever we wanted. And then it was my job to make myself believe all these things, too.

But I couldn't do it. All I could do, when Bill broke the news to me, was cry. And when he told me what the offer was, I only cried harder, because I knew then that we couldn't say no.

It took more than a week before I could trust myself to tell the kids without breaking down. Until then, I shared the news only with Betty, crying my eyes out in her kitchen while the kids were at school. Betty wept a little too, but then, always more stoic than I, she straightened her shoulders. "Of course, there's nothing you can do about it," she said reasonably. "We'll all just have to make the best of it."

Bill and I talked and talked about it, every night after the kids were in bed. Most nights I cried; usually Bill was sympathetic, but other times he grew impatient. "Do you think it's what I want, Ruth?" he asked me.

No, of course not. New Jersey wasn't what any of us really wanted. More built-up and densely populated than Connecticut, it was crisscrossed on the road map with the red and blue lines of highways and turnpikes. Worst of all, it was nearly three hours further from Maine, a hundred and thirty miles in the wrong direction, away from our dream.

"It's not the end of the world. We're still going to build on the lot this year. We promised the kids, and we'll do it. And we won't have to worry quite so much about whether we can afford the lumber to get the place closed in before winter."

"How much vacation do you think you'll be able to take this summer?" I demanded, but I already knew the answer.

"I've told them I need two weeks in August. You know I can't take more than that so soon. But you and the kids can stay at the lake all summer, just like we planned, and I'll drive up every weekend."

"An eight-hour drive is a lot different from five!" I hated the edge in my voice, but I couldn't seem to suppress it. "You'll be so tired you won't get anything done anyway, once you do get there. I don't know how you think we're going to build this year!"

"I'll get the boys going on projects. With you to help them, they can do a lot during the week. And I'll take an extra day or two here and there. We can get a lot done in a long weekend. You'll see."

I wanted to point out that the boys were just children—they were eleven, nine, and eight that spring—but I'd already been amazed at the skills Bill had taught them, at how quickly they'd picked things up. Besides, I was proud of my own carpentry skills— hadn't I just built myself new shelves in the pantry, one day while Bill was at work?—and I didn't want to sell any of us short. If Bill thought the kids and I could build a camp, well, then, we would build a camp.

Some evenings, when I wasn't being stubbornly disheartened and unreasonable, we talked about the future. Bill reminded me that we'd been planning all along to move back to Maine full time, not just for the summers, as soon as we could possibly manage it. While it was true that a move to New Jersey had never been part of our long-range strategy, it was possible that, with his new salary, we could put away enough money for him to think about retiring early. Bill was willing to trade time in Maine now for time in Maine later, he said.

When he put it that way, I felt even worse about acting so sullen. After all, of the two of us, I was certainly getting the better deal—now that we had the lot, and would soon have the camp, I'd be spending all summer on the lake, every year.

So I tried as hard as I could to be as positive as Bill. I agreed that we could all stick it out until he could take early retirement. When we sat down and did the math, figuring on me being able to bring in some additional money by working part time once Leslie was a little older, it looked like that might even be as soon as 1967, as long as Bill found some kind of work to do once we moved back to Maine. That was the year he would turn fifty-five, and Leslie would graduate from high school. Twelve years. It didn't seem so far off, really.

June 17, 1958, Westfield, New Jersey
Ruth

IT IS NOISY IN THE ROOSEVELT JUNIOR HIGH gymnasium, where rows of folding chairs have been set up for the family and friends of the graduating ninth-grade class. A velvet cord denotes the wide sections at the front, to the left and right of the stage, where the graduates will be seated. I can see from the doorway that the first three rows of the center section have signs on them saying they've been reserved, too, I presume for members of the faculty, and the rest of the seats are filling fast when we arrive.

I had hoped to get here earlier. After Steve picked at a plate of macaroni casserole and Jello salad, and after I put him through one final rehearsal of his speech, Leota brought him to the school an hour ago to assemble with his classmates, then came back to the house to collect the rest of us.

I let Leslie put her pajamas on long before dinnertime, trying to think of anything that might give her some comfort, might interrupt her sobbing, and she is staying at home tonight "to look after Grammy." But when I put my head into Lena's room, where the two of them were playing a listless game of "Go Fish," to let her know we were going, she rushed to me and clung to my neck, awash again in tears. It took me some time to get her settled down, and now I think we'll never find seats together for all of us.

But when we enter the gym, the assistant principal meets us just inside door. Awkwardly, he offers me his condolences; he pats Greg and Andy on the head like orphaned puppies. He nods to Leota and Betty, shakes his head as if he still can't believe the news he's heard, and steers us all to the third row of seats, whispering, "We've saved these for your family."

I take the aisle seat, behind Steve's English teacher, Mrs. Best, who turns around in her chair to speak to me, but is overcome and manages after a few moments to sob only, "I'm so sorry, so sorry."

I thank her, then thank her again for the help she gave Steve when he was writing his speech, and say that I hope he'll remember to speak loudly enough so that everyone can hear, something he's had trouble with in practice.

Mrs. Best looks as though she wants to say something else, but she only shakes her head and dabs at her eyes with a limp handkerchief.

I look at my watch; it's a quarter to seven. It stuns me to think that yesterday at this time Bill was still alive. He had just gotten home from New York, had gone upstairs to our room to lie down, instead of getting ready for the Scout meeting, and I was about to drive the boys there myself. I remember again the little flicker of annoyance I felt at the change in plans, and wonder if he noticed it, and wish I could take it back. Not that it would have made any difference, but still.

Andy is next to me, Greg next to him, then Betty and Leota. The rows of chairs behind us are full, but when we sat down, a hush fell over everyone seated in our section, as if they had been waiting to see if we would really be here.

No doubt there are some who think we should have stayed home, but what would we do with ourselves there? Now that the funeral arrangements have been made, the time between now and tomorrow's service stretches like an interminable limbo. I don't even have the cooking and cleaning and laundry to fill the hours, since between Leota and the neighbors, our refrigerator is bulging with food and the bathrooms are sparkling. Each of the kids received a tidy pile of clothing, clean and folded, to take to their rooms before dinner. She's even done the ironing; three nearly-identical white shirts hang in the upstairs hall, in the nook by the window where I keep my sewing machine, ready for the boys to wear tomorrow.

Besides, the program for Steve's graduation was printed last week; he brought one home to show to Bill and me. Now I open the folded sheet of paper the assistant principal handed me when he showed us to our seats, and see, halfway down the page, Steve's name and the title of his speech, "The Teenager as a Citizen."

Long minutes pass. Several people I recognize by sight, and should probably be able to name, pause by my seat to say that they are sorry for our loss. Each time, I feel my throat tighten and I am relieved when I am able to croak out my thanks. Andy's shoulder is pressed against mine, and whenever someone speaks to him, I can feel his whole body shudder with repressed sobs, but I am proud that both he and Greg respond in audible, if cracking, voices to each expression of condolence.

I glance at my watch again and see that it is nearly seven. Did Bill already know what was happening to him by this time yesterday? Had he already begun to call my name?

The music teacher appears from the side door and takes her seat at the sturdy blond upright piano beside the stage. The rustling of programs gradually quiets, she begins to play "Pomp and Circumstance," and we rise as the members of the eighth-grade honor guard lead the graduates down the aisles.

When I see Steve, I am startled at how pale he looks. His face is a white moon floating above the black robe, his brows two black slashes above eyes that seem to have grown larger, darker, rounder overnight.

He doesn't shift his gaze, looking straight ahead, but when he passes the row where we are standing, his fingers brush mine, the lightest touch, to reassure me, or to reassure himself—I am not sure which. Mrs. Best reaches out then and clutches the sleeve of his robe, pulls him toward her and whispers something in his ear, then releases him and presses her handkerchief to her mouth.

Once the graduates have taken their places, the junior high school principal strides to the lectern to welcome us. He looks directly at me, or at least, it feels that way, and for a moment I am afraid he is going to announce Bill's death to the entire audience. I feel certain that everyone already knows, and equally certain that if Mr. Tomlinson says the words, I will have to get up and leave. It will release a flood of pent-up emotion, not only in me, but in the parents and teachers and neighbors filling the seats, a rising river of tears that will carry me out the door of the gym and into the parking lot, where I will sit down on the curb and simply dissolve.

But no, Mr. Tomlinson is speaking only in generalities; he tells us how proud he is of the members of this graduating class and their accomplishments. He thanks the parents for being positive role models, and the teachers for their dedication to their students. He mentions that many Roosevelt Junior High graduates will go on to enroll in honors classes next year at Westfield High School, where he is sure they will continue to excel.

Mr. Tomlinson introduces the city's superintendent of schools, whose speech is mercifully brief, and then it is Steve's turn. I watch him make his way to the aisle from his seat in the middle of the second row of graduates and up the steps to the stage, holding my breath and hoping he won't trip on his robe. At the lectern, he remembers to adjust the microphone before he starts to speak—the superintendent is several inches taller than Steve, who still hopes for a growth spurt before he starts high school.

I hear him thank us all for coming, the teachers and administrators and parents, and I hear the first words of his speech, but after that, after "I am a teenage citizen of Westfield," my mind wanders. I go back to Sunday evening, only two days ago, the last time Steve practiced his speech at home for both Bill and me together.

We had finished supper—just canned tomato soup and toasted cheese sandwiches, because I had cooked a pot roast, potatoes, and vegetables in the pressure cooker for our midday dinner after church—and it was Steve's turn to dry the dishes as I washed them. The other kids had all gone into the living room to watch "Lassie." I could hear the little boy on the show, Timmy, calling to his collie over the music of the theme song.

"I'll dry for you tonight," Bill told Steve. "Why don't you run upstairs and get your speech and let me hear it once more? We won't have time tomorrow, with Scouts."

So Bill and I did the dishes together, our hands or shoulders touching every now and then as I placed a plate or a glass in the drainer and he reached to pick it up. We half-turned from the sink together to watch and listen as Steve delivered his speech. Bill reminded him once to slow down a bit.

When he was finished—it wasn't a long speech—we were only about halfway through the pile of dirty dishes. Bill clapped Steve on the back and told him he'd done a good job.

"Want me to take over drying?" Steve asked.

"I think your mother and I can handle it. Go on and watch television if you want to."

We finished the dishes together, then stood looking out the window over the sink. Bill slipped his arm around my shoulders, and I put mine around his waist and leaned lightly against him.

"The weekends seem to get shorter all the time," he said, and I knew he was thinking about all the things he'd hoped to get done—somehow there was never time for all of them. That afternoon, after dinner, he had lain down on the couch with the Sunday paper and had fallen asleep for over an hour. When he woke up, it was nearly three o'clock, and although he'd changed his clothes and gone outside with the boys then to do some yard work, he had seemed oddly enervated. I'd looked out the window once and seen him leaning against the corner of the garage, watching the boys work.

Uncharacteristically, Bill sighed heavily. I remember that he rubbed his breastbone and said he had a bit of heartburn, that he probably shouldn't have eaten such a big dinner at noon, or lain down so soon afterward.

He was just tired, I thought, from working too hard all week. Sunday evenings were always a little melancholy—Bill preoccupied with the week ahead and thinking about the next morning, about rising early to make his train. On that particular Monday, he would be going first to his office as usual, then heading out on another train at mid-morning for a business meeting in New York City.

I never asked for many details of his work, or his occasional business trips. I knew he was doing well; in only three years with the company, he'd already had two promotions, and at Cooper Alloy, unlike at Pratt and Whitney Machine Tool, annual raises seemed to be taken for granted. Our bank account was gradually growing, and our dream of moving home to Maine once Leslie was through high school appeared to be on track.

Yesterday morning, as I was preparing to leave for the funeral home, I gathered the clothes I had chosen for Bill to be buried in—his best suit, which he had last worn to church on Sunday, and, from his collection of ties, the same flowered one he wore for the formal portrait that I hope will appear with his obituary in the *Bethel Citizen*.

Bill owned a few conservative, solid-colored ties, of course, but the ones we both liked best were the more colorful ones the kids had given him for birthdays and Christmases over the years. Some of their choices bordered on gaudy, but Bill wore them proudly. A few years ago, when we'd had a professional photographer come to the house to take a family portrait, he'd chosen to wear one of the loudest ties in his closet. Even though the photograph was in black and white, the garish vertical stripes, crossed by a wider diagonal slash, stood out against his white shirt and dark suit jacket.

It seemed silly even to worry about what Bill should wear to be buried in, since I had planned a closed casket funeral. Maybe it would have been better to save his best suit, to donate it to the church thrift shop. After all, no one would know if I chose to bury him in the suit with the threadbare lining, or even, for that matter, in the plaid hunting jacket he wore in Maine.

I half considered that for a moment, standing before the open closet, holding one rough wool sleeve against my cheek. After three seasons in the back of the closet, it still smelled of wood smoke and pipe tobacco and, faintly, of sweat. I remembered the last time Bill wore it, last Labor Day morning at the lake, as we packed the cars to head home. How could any of us have known it would be his last day at camp, not just for the year, but forever?

That jacket, I decided, would go back to Maine with us this summer. It would have a place in the back of the tiny closet in our camp bedroom, where it would hold onto Bill's scent, I hoped, forever.

Another scent rose, faintly, as I reached for the hanger that held the jacket of his best suit—peppermint. When I checked the pockets, I found a partial roll of peppermint Tums. There was another roll, also half-gone, in the pocket of the pants he had worn to New York City the day before—the day he came home, went to bed, called me upstairs, and died. I remembered his remark about heartburn after we'd finished the dishes on Sunday evening.

So he'd had at least two days of discomfort. I felt a stabbing pain in my own heart then. If only he had known what was really happening to him—if only he had skipped the business trip to New York and gone to see his doctor instead.

If only he had told me—and not just that vague mention of it as he rubbed his breastbone, but a serious admission: "I'm ill. I don't know what's wrong."

But what would I have said to him in that case? Probably "Take a Tums."

Steve is about halfway through his speech when I realize that, all around me, there are the sounds of sniffling and muted sobs. In the two front rows, nearly all of the teachers—even the men—have brought out tissues or handkerchiefs, and are dabbing their eyes, blowing their noses. Behind us, I can hear quiet sniffs and the occasional masculine honk.

Later, and for years afterward, whenever Leota tells the story of this evening, she will say how proud she was of Steve, how proud his father would have been, how proud and touched everyone was who was there. Then she will reach for her handkerchief, tears welling again in her own eyes, and add, "There wasn't a dry eye in that gym. Not a single dry eye."

When Steve finishes his speech, the applause begins, and lasts for the whole time it takes him to walk back across the stage and down the steps and retake his seat. The music teacher wipes her eyes and begins again to play the piano; the graduates stand and sing. Then the president of the Board of Education, Mr. Merrill, is introduced and hands out the diplomas, shaking each student's hand. I notice that when Steve takes his diploma, Mr. Merrill grips his right hand in both of his and leans in to say something to him.

We all stand as the students process out of the gym, followed by the teachers, and then there is general confusion as the rest of us fill the aisles, waiting to exit the gym.

There is a reception in the cafeteria, where we all go to find our graduates. Most of the kids are standing around in groups, but Steve is alone against one wall. When he sees us, he makes his way over quickly.

"Do we have to stay?" He glances at the table of food. "I'm not hungry."

"Let's get the boys home, Ruth," Leota says gently, and we slip out the door before anyone can detain us.

1955, Newington, Connecticut

Ruth

I WOULD HAVE LIKED TO SAY THAT making a long-range plan for Bill's early retirement—seeing the numbers he scribbled down, and hearing him say he thought it could work—brought an end to my selfish tears, but that wouldn't be true. On bad days, even twelve years still sounded like a lengthy sentence.

The For Sale sign went up in front of our beloved house on Main Street, and it was all I could do not to cry every time I looked out the window and saw it there in the yard.

On a Saturday in the middle of May, Bill and I drove to New Jersey to go house-hunting, leaving the kids at Betty and Elmer's for the day. I cried silently most of the way, as the turnpike carried us south, away from our family and friends in Newington and further from Maine. By the end of the day, we had put down an offer on a house on Fairfield Circle, a quiet residential street in Westfield, but it wouldn't be available for us to move into until the first weekend of September. Bill found an apartment, just a room, really, cheap and sterile, with white walls and a floor painted battleship gray, to rent for the summer. I cried to think of him staying there, all alone, during the week, but he was stoic.

"It won't be bad at all. And I'll be in Maine with you every weekend."

I cried, dabbing my eyes and pretending I had hay fever, when we signed the paperwork that would transfer ownership of our Newington home to a couple with three children. I told Bill that evening that I couldn't see them fitting in with the other families in the neighborhood, that all our neighbors would probably hate us for selling to them. I knew, even as I said it, that it wasn't true—that they were a perfectly nice family; soon the parents would be playing bridge with our friends, and the children would ease seamlessly into the neighborhood gang. But still, I knew the new family couldn't possibly love our house quite the same way Bill and I had, couldn't fill the hole I was sure we would leave in what I had come to think of as the world's most perfect neighborhood. I cried as, while the kids finished out the school year, I packed everything we wouldn't need for the summer into boxes, in preparation for the moving van that would take them away after we returned from Maine on Labor Day weekend.

It would have made more sense, of course, for us to delay heading to Maine for a week or two after school got out, to make time to get things better organized for the move, but Bill didn't suggest it. He knew how eager the kids were to get to the lake. It was as if the camp lot had become their consolation prize, something to make up for the upheaval of the move. And he might have been even more reluctant to suggest it to me; he was still treading carefully around me, trying not to set me off. For my part, I was stubbornly determined to hold him to his promise of the whole summer on the lake for the kids and me, and "the whole summer" meant that we were heading north just as soon as we possibly could.

And so, the Friday after the last day of the school year, Bill, who had been in New Jersey for three weeks by then, coming home only on weekends, arrived at dusk to find me supervising the packing for Maine. A pile of our belongings was stacked almost to the ceiling of the porch, waiting to be loaded into the station wagon.

"I thought we'd do this tomorrow," he suggested. "Let's just relax tonight. It looks like you've gotten a lot done—it will go fast in the morning." He looked longingly toward his favorite chair, which I had pushed up against the wall in a corner of the living room in order to roll up the rug. The house was in a shambles, but what did I care? When we walked out the door the next morning, we wouldn't be back, except for the few days at the end of the summer before we could move into the new house in Westfield.

"I'm planning to be on the road by seven," I replied grimly, ignoring his obvious fatigue at the end of a long work week, and the fact that he had just driven nearly three hours in rush hour traffic on the turnpike to get there.

Bill sighed, took off his jacket and tie, and draped them over the back of his chair. He rolled up the sleeves of his dress shirt, and called for one of the boys to help him carry the camping box from the garage. He had built it a few years earlier, when we'd first bought the old wood-sided Ford station wagon, and he'd made it so that it could be tied securely onto the tailgate when it was folded down. The back window could then be closed down to meet the top of it, although the arrangement wasn't completely air- or water-tight. The gaps around the box resulted in an incessant whistling as we drove, especially at higher speeds, and if it rained, whichever one of the kids was riding in the way-back was tasked with constantly adjusting the rags they packed into the gap to keep as much of the rain out of the car as possible. It gave us room inside for more gear, though, and for the kids. By cramming it full of sleeping bags, camp cookware, and the tent, the six of us had managed to pack for two-week long camping trips in the station wagon.

After several years, Bill had finally gotten tired of constantly having to patch the rotting wooden sides of the 1949 Ford wagon with putty, and he brought home the '53 Chevy wagon from work for me to drive instead. It had been a salesman's car, and I was hesitant about the high mileage, but there was no denying that it was in far better shape than the Ford; at least you couldn't poke your finger through its sides. With the miles he'd be putting on traveling back and forth between New Jersey and Maine, Bill needed something reliable to drive, too, of course, so as soon as he started working in New Jersey, he traded in the crumbling Ford wagon for a green '53 Chevy sedan.

To camp out all summer on the lot, we'd need more gear than we'd ever needed for our previous camping trips, plus several changes of clothes for each of us, books and games, and Leslie's favorite dolls and stuffed animals. Then there were the tools—besides the hammers, handsaws, and Bill's prized electric Skilsaw, we had to make room for garden rakes, shovels, and a hoe, which we'd use to clear and level the lot, as well as two axes, a pickaxe, a mattock, and the bucksaw.

By the time we got both cars loaded, it was late. I had made sandwiches for supper, and a half-dozen more to pack into the cooler in the morning, and I'd saved back just enough milk to pour over cold cereal for breakfast before we got on the road. Before I went to bed, I measured coffee into the percolator, then packed the coffee can into a box with the peanut butter and a few other things that were still left in the cupboards—a can of peaches and one of baked beans, a box of oatmeal, a half-full jar of salted peanuts.

Upstairs, before I got into bed, I parted the curtains and looked out. Across the street in Betty and Elmer's house, all of the windows were dark. Betty had come over earlier with a plate of brownies and we'd said our goodbyes, both of us knowing that although things would never be quite the same again, we would keep our promises to write and call and visit. I might have lost touch with friends from high school, and let my correspondence with college friends dwindle to hastily scribbled notes about our kids on Christmas cards, but for more than a decade now, Betty and I had been as close as sisters. Our Maine roots, our college majors—English—and love of good literature, and our no-nonsense approach to most things had set us apart from many of the other women in the neighborhood, but it was more than that.

Perhaps it was because, like me, Betty was the eldest child and only girl in her family. Like me, she had been given adult responsibilities far too early in her life, and, like me, she had accepted them without question or complaint. For whatever reason, or for so many reasons, we had each found, in the other, the rare, sweet relief of being fully understood.

June 18, 1958, Westfield, New Jersey

Ruth

ON WEDNESDAY MORNING I WAKE UP just as the sky outside my bedroom window lightens to gray. I am surprised to find that I have been asleep, for the first time since Bill's death, although only for an hour or two.

Leslie began the night in her own room, after the rest of us got home from Steve's graduation, after Leota and Betty left to return to Newington for the night. Now, though, she is curled into a tight ball on Bill's side of our bed, and I remember that I was still awake when she tiptoed in around two o'clock and whispered, tearfully, that she couldn't go back to sleep by herself.

When I swing my legs out of bed and begin to stand, I feel a wave of nausea and dizziness. I try to think whether I ate anything yesterday, try to remember what swallowing food feels like, but all I can recall is sips of tea and water, and cups and cups of black coffee.

Neighbors were in and out all day, someone always making a fresh pot. They brought food—cookies and casseroles, muffins and a Jello salad. Leota made sure that Grammy had a sandwich at noon and the kids a snack after school. Everyone offered me food, too, of course, but they accepted my refusal gracefully, each new visitor assuming that the last one had fed me. Winnie, who was there all day, knew better, but after she approached me for the third or fourth time with a plate of crackers or a bowl of soup, I snapped at her, and after that she left me alone.

When I think about putting food into my mouth, chewing and swallowing, it only makes the nausea worse, but I know I need to eat. I'll have to try to force down a piece of toast this morning, and something in the afternoon, or I'll run the risk of passing out later, during the service.

In the kitchen, I am alone in that time before the kids come downstairs, before I peek quietly around the half-open door of

Grammy's room to see if she is awake yet and needs my help. I make coffee, and bring in the morning paper from the front steps.

In large black letters, stark against the newsprint, the headline shouts of a bridge collapse in Vancouver, British Columbia, on Tuesday afternoon. Seventy-nine workers—the bridge was under construction—plunged 175 feet to the waters of the Burrard Inlet. Sixty-one survived and were rescued by fishermen. The others were killed, in the worst bridge disaster in Canadian history.

Eighteen men left their families yesterday morning—kissed their wives, patted their children on the head, chucked their babies playfully under the chin—and never came home again.

Unlike Bill, who died in our own house, in our own bed, with me by his side, these men left their wives to wonder, first, for agonizing hours, if they were among the injured and soggy survivors, and then, for the rest of their lives, how much their husbands had suffered, how they had died—crushed, mangled, drowned?

The sadness of the news story is suddenly too much to bear, and, for the first time, I am crying. Not for myself, I think, not for Bill, but for these Vancouver wives, these other families. I am crying, and I can't stop, my shoulders shaking with sobs, tears falling onto the front page of the *Elizabeth Daily Journal.*

June 1955, Maine

Ruth

IT HAD BEEN GRAY AND DRIZZLING WHEN we left Newington, but as
we drove through Massachusetts, the sun began to poke holes in
the overcast sky. I was being careful, as I had for the whole trip, to
keep Bill's green sedan in sight in front of me, changing lanes
whenever he did. By the time both our cars approached the bridge
from New Hampshire into Maine only puffy fair-weather clouds
remained.

The sun—directly overhead at noon on this, one of the longest
days of the year—beat down relentlessly through the windshield. I
kept the windows down partway as I drove, hoping the fresh air
would prevent the dog, Lucky, from getting carsick. He'd been
curled up on the front seat between Leslie and me for most of the
trip, but now he rode standing on Leslie's lap, front paws on the
passenger door, snuffling with interest at the salt-smelling air.
The tide was out, and mud flats were exposed along both sides of
the channel below the bridge.

The back seat was folded down to accommodate our clothes
and camping gear, and the long handles of the shovels and rakes.
From his cramped nest just behind the front seat, crowded among

duffel bags and boxes, Andy leaned forward to scratch the dog's ears and pointed up through the windshield at the tall green metal bridge.

"See the bridge? When we get to the other side, we'll be in Maine," he told Leslie, whose eyes grew round.

"And then we'll see the sardine man!" she crowed.

"That's right," I said. The forty-foot wooden cutout of a sardine fisherman, clad in yellow slicker and black boots, stood just beyond the bridge in Kittery, beside Route One, welcoming visitors to "Vacationland & Sardineland."

"And then we'll be at the lake!"

"No, we still have two hours to go," Andy corrected her.

In the front seat of Bill's car, just ahead of us, we could see the backs of three heads. As they passed beneath the second of the drawbridge's two tall towers, Greg and Steve turned around to wave at us over the gear that was piled almost to the car's roof on the back seat behind them. Greg pointed upward, to the "Entering Maine" sign mounted on the bridge. We saw him mouth the word, "Maine!" and grin widely.

Bill was relaxing as he drove, with the driver's side window all the way down, elbow resting on the door, shirtsleeve flapping in the breeze. He raised his arm and spread his fingers wide, as if to catch his first handful of Maine air. Tentatively, I unclenched the fingers of one hand from the steering wheel and gave him a cautious wave, knowing he was watching in the rear-view mirror.

Bill had arranged to have several loads of gravel delivered to the lot, widening the road just enough to get both our cars out of the way of anyone who wanted to get by. While the rest of us carried down load after load of our gear, he and Steve pitched the big wall tent on the only remotely level spot, a few yards back from the shoreline. It was a big tent, but when they set up the six old Army cots Bill had picked up somewhere, they took up nearly every inch of space inside it. Bill strung ropes from tree to tree and put up a big tarpaulin under which we could stow all of the gear that wouldn't fit in the tent beneath the cots.

The first load of lumber for the camp had been delivered before we arrived. It was stacked at the top of the steep hill beside the road—two-by-eights for floor joists, two-by-sixes for rafters, two-by-fours for wall studs, and hemlock boards for the floor and for sheathing the roof. Electricity had been brought in the road the year before, and that spring a line had been run to a pole on our lot. Bill dug deep in the camping box and pulled out his Skilsaw and a long extension cord; before suppertime that first night, he and the boys had knocked together a picnic table and benches, and a smaller table where I cooked and heated water for dishes on our two-burner Coleman stove.

June 18, 1958, Westfield, New Jersey

Ruth

THE FUNERAL IS SCHEDULED FOR eight o'clock in the evening. Somehow, we all sleepwalk through the day. I manage to eat some toast at breakfast and the roiling nausea in my belly quiets.

Gradually, the house fills with people. Don's car pulls into the driveway around mid-morning, Leota sitting in the backseat to allow my father to ride up front.

I get up from the table, intending to meet them at the door, but standing too quickly makes me dizzy, and when they enter the kitchen I'm leaning on the back of a chair for support as I feel beads of cold sweat breaking out on my forehead.

"You look terrible, Ruth. Sit down," Leota says brusquely, pulling out another chair and grasping my elbow to guide me into it. Later, she will tell me she feared I would pass out in front of my father, who had been fretting aloud about me incessantly since Don met his plane yesterday, making himself sick with worry.

My father, whom I haven't seen in nearly a year, is sixty-five but looks, today, at least ten years older. For him to have boarded a plane for the first time in his life, within hours of hearing the news yesterday morning, and flown here to be at my side, makes me realize that he understands what a monumental thing this is that has happened.

Of course he does. He was, after all, a year younger than I am now when my mother died unexpectedly and he, too, became a single parent to three small boys and a girl. Why haven't I thought of that before? Of course he would be distraught, reliving my mother's death, which left him solely responsible—as I am—for four young children.

He doesn't know how to give solace; I know this all too well. When my mother died, he retreated into a profound grief from which he has never really emerged. At ten, I turned to him for the comfort and answers that he could never bring himself to give me. What I needed most then was the assurance that he wouldn't let me forget her. Almost as soon as she died, I began to fight a rising panic, seeing right away that my childish memories of my mother were fragile, formless things, without clarity or substance. The more I tried to hold onto them, the more they dissolved, the way a snowflake melted in my hand when I tried to examine it closely.

All I wanted was for him to tell me little things about her—how she parted her hair, what she liked to read, her favorite color—to assure me that what I remembered was true, to fix her in my mind the way she was, a real flesh-and-blood mother, and not just bits of cloud and fog, spun sugar and light, which was how I had come to think of her.

He turned from me then, as he turned from everyone else. If anyone so much as spoke her name to him, if he overheard me say "Mama"—trying to keep her memory alive for Shume and Don, or to make a memory for poor Gib, who would never have even a spun-sugar mother to remember—his face closed and became dark.

And so I learned—we all learned—not to ask for what he couldn't give us. He was a hard worker, morally upright—some would say to a fault—and he provided for us in the ways he could, and left us to figure out the rest.

It made us all rather stiff and serious at home, as if we left our childish selves on the doorstep when we came in from school. We spoke and moved carefully around him, fearing that laughter or commotion of any sort meant disrespect. For the most part, we spoke to him only when he spoke to us.

But today, in spite of the awkwardness that has always existed between us, it is a comfort to have him here, to know that he wishes he could make things better for me, even if he can't say the words. He bends down to my chair and puts his arms around me for a moment, and I feel the smooth skin of his cheek against mine as his dry lips brush my temple.

The Yellow Diamond

Amy

MY MOTHER WAS TEN YEARS OLD when her mother died, leaving her in the care of her father—distant and brokenhearted—and a succession of live-in housekeepers—thoughtless and preoccupied—and in charge, to some extent, of three younger brothers. She had her mother's eyes, her buoyant spirit and sharp wits, and, in a keepsake box on the dresser of her tidy white room, tucked next to an ordinary bobby pin, her mother's yellow diamond ring.

When my grandmother was in the hospital, recovering—so everyone thought—from some sort of unnamed "female trouble," my mother, the oldest child, was allowed a short visit. My grandmother was feeling better—was, in fact, sitting up in a chair when my mother arrived, and she spoke cheerfully of coming home in just a few days. Then she said, "Ruthie, your hair's hanging in your eyes," and lifted her hand to brush back my mother's dark hair. "Here," my grandmother said, and, taking a bobby pin from her own hair, she fastened back the stubborn wisps.

My grandmother relapsed; she hemorrhaged and died the following day.

"I kept that bobby pin for years," my mother told me, not long before her own death. In fact, she said, it had been in her jewelry box for seven decades, disappearing, somehow, only recently.

When, later, my sister and I were sorting through her clothing and jewelry, we ran across several bobby pins, caught in the crevices of drawers or tangled in the chains of necklaces. With each one we found, I caught my breath, wondering...but they all looked the same, and who could tell?

The yellow diamond has a more satisfying story. For a dozen years or more it remained in my mother's keepsake box. I imagine her as a teenager, opening the box every now and then, drawing out the ring and holding it in the palm of her hand.

Perhaps, on an afternoon filled with sorrow and angst and the frustration of being misunderstood, she escaped to her room and slipped the ring onto her finger, holding it up to the light, gazing at the yellow stone through angry adolescent tears.

Perhaps, preparing for a high school dance, with no one to help her dress and her awful state of motherlessness suddenly overwhelming her, she put on the ring and felt, almost, my grandmother's cool hands lifting the hair from the nape of her neck to hook the tiny clasp of her dress.

In the mid-1940s my mother, newly married herself, gave her mother's ring to my Uncle Don, her second brother, so that he and his sweetheart, Leota, could become engaged before he was sent overseas during World War II. Many years later, my aunt and uncle returned the yellow diamond, now set in a gold pendant, to my mother, and she often wore it on a chain around her neck.

My mother had only ten short years with her mother. I am fortunate to have had more than four decades with mine. While most of my mother's memories of her mother were half-formed impressions, freeze-frames from her very young childhood, my own mother's strength and resilience shaped my personality and my life in ways I am still only beginning to discover.

When something in my life requires a decision, she often weighs in to help me make it. I know when what I've done would make her proud, and when I've done something that would warrant her disapproval. Two decades after her death, I still converse with her in my mind, and, sometimes, I find it easier to write her part of our dialogue than my own.

I have the yellow diamond pendant now. And now and then, on an afternoon filled with sorrow and angst and the frustration of being misunderstood, when my awful state of motherlessness overwhelms me, I escape to my room, take out the yellow diamond on its gold chain and feel, almost, my mother's cool hands lifting the hair from the nape of my neck to hook the tiny clasp.

June 18, 1958, Westfield, New Jersey

Ruth

DON SITS DOWN IN THE KITCHEN CHAIR next to mine and pulls me into his arms. Neither of us speaks. Tears course down his cheeks and land on the shoulder of my blouse, but I don't move for a long, long time.

Later, after many more cups of hot black coffee, someone hands me a cup of broth instead, and I sip it slowly. It's warm and rich, and I wonder who brought it, thinking to myself that it is someone who understands grief. Someone, a neighbor, maybe, or a friend from church, knows instinctively that a cup of hot broth can be exactly the thing that is needed at a time like this: the medicine of comfort and sustenance.

Betty and Elmer arrive in the mid-afternoon. Elmer looks terrible, like a man who has just lost his best friend, which, of course, is just what he is. When I see him, I feel suddenly that I have been selfish, thinking only about what Bill's death means for me.

After a brief hug, Elmer quickly finds himself a project that needs doing in the backyard. Betty wants to discuss the logistics of how the boys and I will get to Bethel for the burial. She's afraid I might have some idea of making the drive myself, in our car, and she wants to make sure she registers her opinion that that is out of the question.

I tell her I'm going to drive to Newington tomorrow with the boys, spend the night at Don's, and we'll all ride to Maine on Friday with him and my father. But both Betty and Don veto this plan, and Don tells me I won't be driving anywhere, that we'll all ride with him to Newington tomorrow.

Although I'm having trouble thinking clearly about how many passengers there will be, and how many seats there are in Don's car, I'm certain there isn't enough room. Besides, I tell him, that will mean he has to drive the boys and me all the way back to Westfield on Saturday, then turn around and drive back home to Newington.

He says he doesn't care a thing about that, so long as I understand that I won't be driving anywhere, but he does agree that we can take my car, leaving his at our house until he brings us back. Then Betty says she and Elmer will take Greg and Andy back home with them after the funeral tonight, and bring them to Don's house tomorrow when we arrive there. This plan seems to make the most sense to everyone, and will free up Greg and Andy's room tonight so that Don and Leota can sleep there. I'll put my father in Leslie's room and let her sleep in my bed, since that's where she's bound to end up anyway.

I'll need to strip the beds and make them up with clean sheets, tidy up Leslie's toys, make room in the boys' closet for Don and Leota to hang their things. I go upstairs to get started, but the discussion has exhausted me, and even though I have a houseful of company and it doesn't seem like the right thing to do, I go instead to my own room to lie down.

Despite the rise and fall of voices downstairs and the sun shining through the bedroom window, I fall soundly asleep almost as soon as I stretch out on the bed. A half hour later, I wake with a start; I've been dreaming that I am at the lake, searching for Bill in the woods behind the camp, thinking that if only I have enough time before dark, I will find him there.

1955, North Pond, Woodstock, Maine

Ruth

EARLE PALMER AND HIS CREW FROM the Mann Company had harvested all of the marketable hemlocks and pines along the east shore before dividing it up into camp lots. When we arrived on the last Saturday of June in 1955, to spend our first full summer on the lake, the logs had been trucked to the mill, but tops and branches littered the lot. Before the day was over, Bill had built a sawbuck out of two-by-fours, and he and the boys began sawing the limbs into pieces to burn for campfires, using the old buck saw with its heavy iron frame and three-and-a-half-foot blade.

Except for a quick swim to cool off in the late afternoon, there was no time to rest. Besides the two rough tables, one for cooking and one for eating, and the two benches that could be used at the picnic table or dragged to the edge of the firepit, they built a small lean-to shed to keep our tools out of the weather. Steve helped Bill pitch the tent and we all carried down sleeping bags, cots, and duffle bags from the car.

Then they began to haul the remaining brush into the woods at the edge of the lot to molder away, but that still left the problem of the stumps. Bill had had the idea that, armed with shovels and hand tools, he and the boys could do most of the necessary site preparation, but their first attempt to dig out a two-foot-diameter stump convinced him otherwise.

The next afternoon, a Sunday, he set off for town on a quest to find, on short notice, a bulldozer operator who was not otherwise engaged. On the recommendation of a friend—"he does good enough work when he's sober"—and much to my chagrin, he hired Jack, whose easy availability was his greatest asset.

Jack showed up the next morning, about an hour later than they had arranged. Having been warned by Bill that there was no place on the camp road to turn around with a truck and trailer, he had unloaded his bulldozer at the end of the road and driven it the mile in. When he arrived, Leslie and I were at the top of the hill beside the road, rummaging through the back of the station wagon, which we were using to store the boxes of food I was afraid would attract bears if left out. It was a chilly morning, and we were searching for dry milk and cocoa powder so I could make hot chocolate for the kids.

We heard the dozer coming from a long way off, a rumbling and clanking that grew louder as it rounded the curve in the road by the Bickford and Baldwin camps, continued past the Lambs' lot, and chugged into view.

"Lord, I hope no one on this lake was trying to sleep in this morning," I called down to Bill.

"Are we almost to Augusta?" Jack shouted cheerfully from the seat of his clanking machine, which belched out a puff of black smoke every few seconds. "Bill told me it was a mile in this road, but I gotta say, that's about the longest goddamned mile I've ever driven!"

I winced and glanced down at Leslie, who was staring, transfixed, at the enormous machine. Behind Jack, his feet braced on the hitch that protruded from the back of the dozer, a younger man was clinging to the backrest of the operator's seat with hands the size of small hams.

Bill climbed the hill to meet them at the road, and Jack slid down from the seat of the bulldozer to shake hands. He held out his hand to me, and I took in his ragged, grimy fingernails, tobacco-stained whiskers, and missing front teeth. As I stepped forward to shake his hand, a powerful reek of stale beer and even staler perspiration wafted toward me.

"And how's this little lady this morning?" Jack asked Leslie. As he bent to offer her his hand, I shot a scathing look in Bill's direction, but he pretended not to notice.

The boys appeared at the top of the hill, and Jack greeted them enthusiastically. "Nice-looking family you've got here," he told Bill, his gaze sweeping over all of them, and lingering on me for longer than I liked. "Hard workers, too, I bet," he added approvingly. He turned back to the dozer. "You gonna get off of there, Dub?" he shouted to the other man, who climbed cautiously down and stood in the road, looking down at his shoes.

"That's my brother's boy, Darrell," Jack told us. "He's slow, and he don't hear very good, so if you got anything to tell him, make sure you holler loud. He's pretty good help, though. Strong as a bull."

He climbed back up to his perch. I grasped Bill's sleeve and pulled him several yards away to hiss in his ear.

"You've gone and hired a drunk! And don't say you can't smell it on him!"

"It's Monday morning, Ruth. He may be a little hung over from the weekend, that's all."

"And did you hear him swearing? I don't want that around the kids!"

"Oh, well, I don't imagine that's anything they haven't heard before. Besides, I didn't have much of a choice. The other two guys I went to see yesterday were booked up till August, and we can't do anything else until we can get these stumps out of here."

I set my mouth in a straight line of disapproval and told Leslie to get ready to go. "We're going to Bethel for groceries," I announced.

"What about our hot chocolate?"

"Never mind that now."

"But I want to watch the bulldozer."

"They'll still be working when we get back."

"Please, Mommy!"

"We'll watch them dig out one stump, but then we're going."

Bill helped Jack negotiate the steep bank with the bulldozer and they got right to work. Armed with mattock and pickaxe, Bill and Darrell chopped through the large tree roots. The boys, eager to be part of the action, tossed aside their sweatshirts and raced back and forth, carrying branches to the brush pile and looking for anything else they could do to help.

They all stood back while Jack got his machine into position, one corner of the wide blade wedged beneath the stump. He threw the dozer into low gear and slowly ground it forward, at the same time expertly working the levers that lifted the blade, and plucked the stump from the ground like a wisdom tooth. Everyone cheered.

"Slick as a goddamned whistle!" Jack hollered over the racket. I felt myself cringe, and I hustled Leslie back up the hill to the car.

The first thing I noticed when Leslie and I returned was the absence of noise. Instead of the grinding of gears and clanking of treads I had been expecting to hear when I opened the car door, there was silence, then Jack's voice, loud enough to carry up to the road and beyond.

"Goddamn it all to hell!"

Beside me in the passenger seat, Leslie gasped. I slammed my door shut before we could hear any more, but Leslie already had hers flung open and was climbing out.

Jack, Darrell, Bill, and the three boys stood around the bulldozer, gazing dolefully at one of the enormous jointed metal treads, which lay on the ground beside the machine, dangling uselessly from one wheel. Leslie hurried down the hill to join her brothers.

"What happened?"

"She threw a tread," Greg said knowledgeably.

"Who did?"

"The bulldozer."

"Why's the bulldozer a girl?"

"Because she's nothin' but goddamned trouble!" Jack interjected before Greg could respond.

"Oh."

"Leslie, come help me carry down the groceries," I called. "You boys, too. Right now!"

Bill and Jack began to discuss how best to get the tread back on the machine, and to try one idea after another. Before long the air was turning blue with Jack's curses, and Bill had added a few milder ones of his own, but no progress had been made. As I made my way down the hill with the last sack of groceries, I looked down and saw Jack slip a metal flask from his pocket, remove the cap, and surreptitiously take a swallow.

I grasped Leslie by the hand and pulled her roughly toward the table beneath the canvas tarp Bill had strung up for an awning, where I had set up a rudimentary camp kitchen.

"Come on," I said. "We're going to pack a lunch so the boys can take a picnic to Rock Island."

I began to hastily slap together peanut butter and jelly sandwiches, wrapping them haphazardly in waxed paper and tossing them into the wicker picnic hamper, along with a thermos of lemonade, a packet of cookies, and the quart of potato salad I'd intended to serve with hamburgers for supper.

"Can I go, too?" Leslie asked.

"You can *all* go," I said tersely.

In ten minutes flat I had bundled them into the flat-bottomed wooden boat, tossing their orange life preservers in after them, instructing Andy to make sure Leslie was properly buckled into hers. I sent them on their way, the noise of the ancient motor, I hoped, drowning out Jack's curses.

An hour or so later, when the kids returned from their picnic, the tread was back on the dozer. The men were working side by side, as smoothly as if they'd worked together as a three-man crew all their lives.

Bill and Darrell were alternating heavy blows with the pickaxe and the mattock to chop through the roots, some as thick as a man's arm, the tools making steady, rhythmic thunks. High off the ground, from his seat behind the controls, Jack methodically dug up the stumps with the blade, then tumbled them end over end across the lot to the growing pile at the edge of the woods.

Darrell was eating a peanut butter sandwich, which he stuffed, unwrapped, into his pants pocket in order to free up both hands to wield the mattock. Once he was done chopping, he'd step back, wipe his brow, pull out the sandwich, and take a bite or two while Jack pushed out the stump. Leslie watched, fascinated, as he picked bits of lint from his pocket off the mangled sandwich before taking a bite. Then he returned it to his pocket and, armed with a peavey and a pulp hook, he and Bill helped to guide each stump to the pile ahead of the blade.

June 18, 1958, Westfield, New Jersey
Ruth

LATE IN THE DAY, AFTER SOMEONE HAS warmed an array of casseroles in the oven and set them on the kitchen table, and everyone but me has picked at them halfheartedly, and someone else has put them all away and done up the dishes, Leslie slips out of Lena's room and into the kitchen.

Without being asked, the kids have all taken turns spending time with their grandmother today, in the sunroom we converted to a bedroom when she broke her hip last year, and we had to fetch her down from Maine to stay with us. I don't think there has been much talking; they've sat quietly with her, sometimes holding her thin hand.

Bill's sister, Kaye, and her husband, John, a Baptist preacher, have flown in today; they'll go to the funeral, and tomorrow morning they'll take Lena back to Texas with them on the plane. No one has asked me if this is what I want. There's an unspoken consensus that I have too many other things, too many other people, to take care of, without being asked to look after a frail old lady with a shattered hip that will never fully heal.

"Mommy, Grammy wants to talk to you," Leslie says.

My mother-in-law is in her wheelchair, so small and slumped down so low that she looks like a child. I go to her and automatically slip my hands under her arms to raise her, adjusting the pillow behind her back.

"I think I'd like to just get into bed, Ruth," she says. We've already discussed the funeral, and she has told me, in no uncertain terms, that she will not be going. I don't know if she wants to spare us the challenge of transporting her, with her chair, to the church, getting her unloaded and up the steps to the door, or if she can't bring herself to go because she is overwhelmed with sadness and wants only to curl inward and let her grief wash over her. But I've learned not to argue with her when her mind is made up, so last night, when she told me what she had decided, I only nodded.

I pull down the bedspread and sheet, and help her from the chair to the bed. With her arms around my neck, I feel again that brief, longed-for sense of being mothered, while at the same time I am reminded of lifting my children, placing them gently in their beds, trying not to wake them after they'd fallen asleep on the couch or in the car.

When she is settled in bed against the pillows and I straighten up as if to step away, she beckons with her hand for me to lean closer. Her eyes are red-rimmed, the thin skin below them shiny and bluish.

"Kaye is taking me to Texas to live with her," she says, so softly that I can't tell if it's a statement or a question.

I nod. "Yes."

"That's all right, then. That will be all right."

"Are you sure?" Until last year, I think she could count on her fingers the number of trips she'd made outside of Maine in her lifetime, and I know how much she's been looking forward to our summer at camp, only a few miles from her hometown, to visits with her friends, and with the two of her sisters, Marjorie and Grace, who still live in the Bethel area.

She's only begun to get used to the New Jersey climate, to remember that she doesn't need to put on a sweater and a warm hat to have her morning coffee on the porch in June. I can tell that life in our suburban town, where the houses are closer to the street and to each other than she's been accustomed to, still makes her nervous. It took months for her to stop rolling her chair to the window every time she heard a siren, or calling to me whenever she heard a child's raised voice outside. What will she think of Texas, the heat, and Kaye and John's chaotic household?

But she smiles bravely at me, nods. "You've taken such good care of me for a long time. It's Kaye's turn now."

"You can teach her girls to cook." My throat swells; my voice is thick. She loves to sit by our kitchen window, directing from her chair as Leslie learns to make a simple supper or a one-egg chocolate cake. They were going to start on pies soon, I remember, and I make a mental note to teach Leslie how to make a good piecrust. Lena is famous for her pies, which she made by the hundreds during the more than two decades after Bill's father died, when she and her mother kept body and soul together by running their small restaurant in Bethel.

The memory of my first visit to Farwell & Wight's Tea Room, the October before Bill and I were married, is still detailed and clear in my mind. The air was clean and crisp, just as it should be on an early October day in Maine, and the maples along Church Street were brilliant with fall color. Bill had brought me to Bethel to meet his mother and grandmother for the first time. I was nervous, but I hardly had time to think about it; we hadn't been in the restaurant for more than five minutes that Saturday afternoon when a large group of autumn tourists made its way from the train station up Main Street, in search of a meal and a piece of homemade pie.

There were only Lena, her mother, Addie, who was already over eighty by then, and Ruby, their hired girl, to cope with the crowd. They bustled back and forth from kitchen to table, always smiling, as they juggled plates laden with hot turkey sandwiches, meat loaf and mashed potatoes, lemon meringue pie. Leaving Bill at the counter with his mug of coffee, I slipped through the swinging door to the kitchen, found an apron in the first place I looked, hanging on a nail beside the door, and attacked the mounting pile of unwashed dishes.

"I want to tell you something," Lena says. She pats the edge of her bed, and I perch there, hoping whatever she has to say won't make us late for the funeral, even though I know I've allowed plenty of extra time.

"What is it?" I try to smile at her, and she takes my hand in both of hers. Her fingers are cool and bony.

"Do you know how old I was when Bill's father died?" she asks me. "I was thirty-eight, just like you. You didn't know that, did you?"

I've never really thought about it. As sturdy and active and capable as she had been at fifty-six, when I first knew her, she was always Bill's mother, and I'd never considered that she'd ever been my own age. I shake my head.

"It was a hard time," she says, and her eyes, behind the lenses of her glasses, have a faraway look. "Kaye was such a little girl, you know, not even three. I didn't know what to do. I thought it was the end of the world. And then, when we'd hardly buried Walter, Papa died."

I can only imagine the grief with which Bill, at twelve, must have struggled, losing his father, then, only nine days later, his grandfather. The family must have reeled for months from the double blow.

"But it was not the end of the world. Do you hear me? I was young and strong, and I had my children. I had to make a life for them, so that's what I did. And after a time—I won't say it was a short time, and I won't say it wasn't a hard time, but after a time—I realized I had also made a life for myself."

It is more than she has said since Bill died, and she closes her eyes, as if the words have exhausted her. Her eyelids, like the paper-thin skin beneath her eyes, look purple, like bruises. For a moment I think she has fallen asleep, and I start to withdraw my hand, but she grips it tighter, opens her eyes.

"Kaye is my daughter." I can see that she is struggling to find the words to tell me something, unaccustomed as she is—as we all are, really, we stoic Mainers—to any display of emotion.

I wait.

"You're my daughter, too, Ruthie."

She's never called me anything but just plain Ruth before; no one has, not for years, except, occasionally, my father or one of my brothers, who still remember when I was little Ruthie, in pigtails and pinafores, before my mother died, before I grew tall and brisk and self-sufficient.

"I love you, Mum," I surprise myself by saying, using Bill's name for her, as I bend to kiss her wet cheek. Kaye and John will leave tomorrow, taking her with them, and I don't know when—or even if—I'll see her again.

The boys are standing in a stiff row at the foot of the stairs, their hair damp and combed, their ties straight, their shoes—I note with approval—shined and buffed. Joan Sweet has already been here to collect Leslie, who has been deemed too young and too fragile to attend the funeral. She's been crying almost non-stop for the nearly two days since Bill's death; she spent most of her last day of school, yesterday, with her head buried in her arms on her desk.

I felt dreadful when her teacher called after school yesterday to express her condolences, and to tell me what a difficult day Leslie had had. I knew then that it had been a terrible thing to let her go to school, to do nothing to stop her when she came downstairs, dressed in a blouse and jumper, her saddle shoes dangling by their laces in one hand, and sat on a kitchen chair to put them on.

It would have taken only a word from me to send her back upstairs to change out of her school clothes. But I simply told her that she looked nice, and sent her into the bathroom to brush her hair. I poured cereal into her bowl and set a glass of orange juice at her place.

Winnie is here to drive us to the funeral home. We'll take our car because the boys would be cramped in the backseat of her little Rambler, but I've agreed to let her drive us. Don and Leota, Betty and Elmer will all go in Don's car, leaving Elmer's and Winnie's cars in our driveway.

One of the many pieces of advice I received from Mr. Gray yesterday was to be sure not to leave the house looking unoccupied during the funeral, in case thieves had been reading the death notices.

"People can be so unscrupulous," he said sadly.

The *Westfield Leader* with the notice of Bill's death won't be out until tomorrow, and I doubt if any thief who reads the *Hartford Courant* would drive a hundred miles to rob our house, but I didn't bother to point this out to Mr. Gray. I had caused him to sigh and shake his head so many times already.

Winnie precedes us out the side door, followed by Steve, then Greg. At the last moment, as I'm taking a quick glance around the kitchen, patting my purse to be sure I have tissues and gloves, touching my head to see if I put on my hat, or only thought I did, Andy turns to look back at me.

"Are we going to leave Grammy all alone?" His eyes are wide, almost panicked, his voice anguished.

All at once, I know what he is telling me without saying the words: "I can't do this—please don't make me do this."

"Would you prefer to stay with Grammy?" I ask, making my voice as gentle as I can. He bursts into tears, nodding.

"I think that would be very nice of you," I tell him, and he rushes past me, back inside. He looks back once, grateful and relieved, and slips through the open door of his grandmother's room.

1957–1958

Ruth

FOR MORE THAN TWENTY YEARS, until Bill's grandmother, Addie, whom we all called Gram, was eighty-four years old, she and her daughter Lena ran their small restaurant in Bethel. Famous for their breads, pies, and home-cooked meals, they also served as a stop on the Maine Central Bus Line for boarding students traveling to and from nearby Gould Academy and the many tourists who came to visit the picturesque New England village, staying at the stately Bethel Inn, or with local friends and relatives.

They sold the restaurant in the mid-1940s, a few years before Gram passed away. After her mother's death, Lena lived with her sister and brother-in-law, Grace and Ernest Buck, in their big house on Railroad Street for most of the year. Each winter, in early- to mid-January or so, Bill drove to Maine and brought her back with him to Newington, and later Westfield, where she stayed with us for two months, or longer if Maine was having a particularly hard winter.

It wasn't always easy. In the kitchen, Lena was used to being the boss, and, while I welcomed an extra pair of hands when it came to peeling potatoes or washing dishes, her take-charge attitude often tested my patience. If I had been out, visiting with Betty or running an errand, and came home to find that she had started dinner without asking what I had planned, or if she nearly elbowed me out of her way to take over some task because she knew a better way to do it, it was hard not to feel annoyed, and often I didn't try very hard to hide it.

Once, when we had had a particularly challenging afternoon, and she had gone to her room to rest before dinner, I met Bill at the door when he arrived home from work and lit into him before he'd even had a chance to put down his briefcase. It was "your mother this" and "your mother that"; I was nearly weeping with frustration.

At first I could see that Bill was trying to be sympathetic, but when a small smile began to play around his lips, I became even more agitated.

"I'd like to know what you find amusing about this!" I snapped.

"I was just thinking about something I heard back home, when I worked those couple of years in the logging camps." He was smiling broadly now, the corners of his eyes crinkling. "They used to say, 'You can take a hundred men and put them in a lumber camp in the woods for the whole winter with no problems, but you can't *build* a house big enough for two women!'"

In the early fall of 1957 Lena, who was then seventy-two, tripped and fell outside of Grace's home, shattering her hip. Suddenly, it was clear to all of us that she would be unable to take care of herself any longer. Grace and Ernest, though a few years younger, were themselves well along in years, and not in a position to care for an invalid.

Bill's only sibling, Kaye, was living in Texas with her family. Except for her visits with us during the winter months, Lena had never lived anywhere but Maine, had rarely even ventured as far from home as Portland. Even New Jersey seemed like another world to her, but it went without saying that she would be brought there to live full-time with us. That was what family was for.

As soon as the doctor said her hip was healed enough to allow her to travel, Bill and I drove to Maine to get her, bringing Andy, who was ten, along. At the time, it seemed to us as if, after two years, he was still struggling, more than the other kids, with the move to New Jersey and the adjustment to a new neighborhood and school. He needed some individual attention, something it was nearly impossible to give to the third of four children born within six years. We thought it would be good for him, being the one chosen to accompany us, while the others stayed behind, to be looked after overnight by the Sweets.

And it was good, in a way. During the eight-hour ride to Bethel, Andy talked more than he ever did at home, telling us things he hadn't had a chance to say at the dinner table. It was good for us, too; we'd so seldom had a chance to give our undivided attention to only one of our children, and it may have been the first time we really understood just how intelligent, thoughtful, and sensitive our third son was.

But the ride back to New Jersey the following day was hard for all of us; certainly it was most grueling of all for Lena, who, unable to sit upright, rode stretched out on a thin mattress in the back of our new station wagon, with the back seat folded down. Bill and I hadn't comprehended just how much pain she was in, until we turned south onto Route 26 from Railroad Street and bumped across the train tracks. She didn't complain—she was Lena, after all—but we heard her draw in her breath sharply and saw her wince. For the four hundred miles between Maine and New Jersey, each jolt and jiggle—and there were thousands—was agony for her. Andy rode beside her, sitting cross-legged or curled up, holding her hand, and he seemed near tears for much of the trip, looking as helpless as Bill and I felt.

Between her winter stays in Newington and our occasional trips to Bethel before we started to build the camp, two years before she broke her hip, the kids had all grown quite close to their grandmother, but not in the same way they did after we brought her to live with us. Lena and Andy, especially, forged a bond as they rode in the back of the station wagon that day, both holding their breath each time the car encountered road construction, closing their eyes together, each tightly gripping the other's hand.

Throughout the months since then, as she had become a part of their daily lives, each of the kids had developed a special relationship with Grammy. She taught Leslie to cook and bake, and to mend a torn seam with tiny, even stitches, and she took great pride in the achievements of all the boys. But when we gathered for meals, it was Andy who sat next to her at the table, who filled her water glass from the cut-glass pitcher that was too heavy for her to lift, and carefully placed child-sized servings of roast chicken and mashed potatoes on her plate. Whenever she began to tell us a story about the restaurant, or about growing up in Maine, or about Bill's antics as a child, it was Andy to whom her eyes went first.

Grammy
Steve, Greg, Andy, Leslie, Amy

Amy: After Gram Farwell died, and before Grammy broke her hip and came to stay with you for several months, until Dad died, did Grammy live with Grace and Ernest in Bethel, but come to Newington (and then Westfield) for most of the winter? That's what I seem to remember Mom telling me. Did Dad drive to Bethel to get her and bring her back? Did any of you ever go along?

Greg: I remember Dad going to get her after she broke her hip, but I have no memory of her in Newington.

Andy: I am not sure about Grammy coming to Newington during the winters, or where she was living in Bethel, but with Aunt Grace and Uncle Ernest makes sense. I do know that she broke her hip in the fall of 1957 and Dad, Mom, and I went to Maine to bring her to Westfield. We must have gotten there late and stayed overnight at the camp on Friday night. Saturday morning Dad took the buck saw and axe; he handed me the .22 rifle and a box of .22 "shorts." We went into the wood slash up behind the camp. He cut some firewood and told me I could shoot squirrels. No squirrels around, but I shot some old beer cans. Then we went and saw Grammy. Sunday morning, we put Grammy in the station wagon and drove her to Westfield. She was in pain and very uncomfortable. I squeezed into the space behind the front seat and rode there.

Steve: I'm sure that Grammy lived in Newington with us sometimes, mostly because I remember a time when Dad came home from work and Mom went into a tirade about some issue she had with Grammy that day.

Andy: I just remembered a story from Newington when I was about three or four. Grammy was visiting for a while. She loved apples, and had a bowl of them with a paring knife for peeling on her dresser. Apparently, I climbed up on her dresser and attempted to peel an apple for myself. Slash—blood—rush to the doctor for stitches. I have the scar to show for it.

Amy: There was a funeral in New Jersey, then a committal service in Bethel, right? I knew Dad died in New Jersey and was buried in Bethel, but I guess I never thought about the logistics. Where did Grammy go when you all came to Maine? Did she go out to live with Auntie Kaye and Uncle John right away at that point?

Greg: Some answers, and some poor recollections...I believe Kaye and John came right away to take Grammy to live with them in Texas. She had broken her hip about a year before and came to live with us. She was bedridden at first, then in a walker. I can't recall if we went to Maine just for the burial, then came back, then went back again shortly; I think so.

Leslie: I did not attend the funeral, or go to Maine for the burial. I stayed with the Sweets for both. So yes, you guys did come back for me after the burial. Then we went to Maine shortly after that.

Andy: Guess we did a lot of road time back and forth to Maine in 1958. Did Mom do all that driving?

Steve: I guess Mom must have done the driving. Heck, she did everything! I seem to remember driving some stretches of the Maine trip on a learner's permit (thankfully I wasn't stopped!), but that must have been after I turned at least fifteen!

Andy: Grammy was living with us with her broken hip and sleeping in the first floor sun room. I didn't know Leslie went to the Sweets' house during the funeral; I thought I was the only one who did not go to the church. What happened for me was that we were all ready to go and heading out the door and I said to Mom, "Are we going to leave Grammy all alone?"

Mom must have realized I was freaked all over, so she said, "Would you prefer to stay with Grammy?"

So I did. Lots and lots of times I have recalled how gently considerate and thoughtful Mom was under those circumstances. I regret not ever talking to her enough about those days—it makes me miss her now all over again. And again, I think about how difficult death was/is to talk about. Grammy and I sat together while everyone was at the service. We played cribbage (she always beat me) and did not speak about Dad's death. We kept our feelings to ourselves, I guess. At that point I couldn't have expressed mine anyway.

June 18, 1958, Westfield, New Jersey
Ruth

AT THE FUNERAL HOME, BEFORE THE service begins, I am patted and hugged and spoken to in hushed tones by many people; afterward I will remember almost none of their words and gestures. Nor will I remember much about the service itself—the minister's words, what hymns are sung. I will remember instead how a gap in the maroon curtains, closed over the tall windows on the west side of the chapel to block the rays of the setting sun, allows a narrow shaft of light to fall in front of the altar. From the first row, where I am seated between Steve and Greg, I could almost put out my hand and touch it, could almost reach to gather the light into my palm. I watch the dust motes that swirl slowly within it, thinking again, as I have so many times over the past two days, where are you now, Bill?

I am startled when the minister declares from the pulpit, loudly, "Dust thou art, and unto dust thou shalt return."

But Reverend McCorison is wrong, I think. If Bill were here, he wouldn't be the swirling dust. He'd be that piercing shaft of light.

In spite of the short notice, several of Bill's friends from school have driven down from Bethel for the funeral. I made only two phone calls to Maine the evening he died: one to my youngest brother, Gib, who still lives near our father in Bangor, and the other to Lena's sister Grace in Bethel. I left it to Gib to let my father know, and to Grace to spread the word among Bill's family and friends as she saw fit.

So I am surprised to see how many have made the long drive. From Bangor, only my father is here; Gib, unable to miss the three days of work the trip would have required, will meet us in Bethel on Saturday. But from Bethel, there are several. To represent the family, Bill's cousin Bucky, Grace's son who runs the Shell station and the Western Auto store, is here, along with his brother, Raymond. They've ridden down with Pete Chapin and Herbie

Rowe, Bill's closest friends from his days at Gould Academy, with whom he used to "raise Cain," as Lena has told me more than once.

If you took a picture of the four of them, seated in a row in a pew near the back, in the stiff dark suits that have no doubt hung in their closets since the last time they attended a funeral, you would capture four matching expressions of utter shellshock. If Bill had been killed by a falling tree in a woods accident, or had died in a farm tractor rollover, they could accept it. But for one of their own to be felled, at Bill's age, by a bad heart? It doesn't seem possible, and it makes them question their own presumed immortality.

Betty and Elmer are seated directly behind me, sharing a pew with Don and Leota, and each of them has kept a hand on one of my shoulders throughout the service. At times I've thought that without the light pressure of Betty's fingers or the heavier warmth of Elmer's palm to ground me, I might float from my seat on the velvet-cushioned pew and swirl like the dust motes in the shaft of light from the window.

We all rise at the first organ strains of the final hymn, then take our seats again as Reverend McCorison draws the service to a close with a prayer. The organist begins to play again, softly. The music is soothing, slow, but, I am relieved to realize, not a traditional funeral march.

Among the dozens of questions Mr. Gray asked me yesterday was, "Is there a particular piece of music you would like for the recessional?"

At first I shook my head, told Mr. Gray just to select something appropriate; whatever he chose would be fine. But then, as I was nearly ready to leave, I remembered my mother's funeral, and the haunting dirge—so dreary, so final—that floated down from the organ pipes at the rear of the church as we filed by her casket. Chopin's famous funeral march. How many times have I left a church funeral to the bleak strains of that same music?

"About the music for the recessional."

Mr. Gray paused, his pen hovering over the forms he'd been filling out. "Yes?"

"Not that Chopin piece. Please."

"No?" I saw him draw a line through something he'd written. "Is there another piece you'd prefer, then?"

"Well, no, but—"

How to tell him what it was that I wanted the music to convey? I thought of the boys, of how they would hear the music as they laid their hands on the lid of the closed casket to say goodbye to their father. Of how—even if they didn't think they remembered it—when they heard it again, someday, at another funeral, they would be brought back here to this church, to this day, in an instant. Just as I had slipped back, time and again, into that frightened, ten-year-old, motherless girl.

"I'd like something—something with a little—"

"Yes?"

"Oh, something with a little *hope*, I suppose. For my children."

"Hope." Mr. Gray seemed to be printing the word in the margin of his form.

"It's just that funeral music always seems so bleak, and—well—really, it's still springtime—"

"Yes. Springtime. Well. Yes. But we won't want something too *sprightly*, I'm sure." He cocked his head slightly, questioning.

"Oh, no. Not sprightly. No. Just—maybe just not too terribly gloomy? Not what you'd call a—a dirge?"

"No dirge." He made another note in the margin. "I'll see what I can find."

He's done well. I consult the program, hastily typed by Mr. Gray's secretary this morning, and mimeographed in blurred purplish ink onto thin paper. The music is Pachelbel, the Canon in D Major. It's perfectly appropriate for a funeral, certainly nothing that could be called "sprightly." It is quiet, soothing, and yet the notes slide over each other like a stream flowing to the sea, moving up and down the scale with enough vigor that—if I weren't sitting here, at the funeral of my husband, flanked by my two eldest children, with a crowd of people behind me waiting to murmur their condolences—I might, in fact, hear a hint of hopefulness, of renewal.

I close my eyes for a moment, and when I open them again, a dark-suited usher has paused at the end of our pew, waiting for Steve and Greg to escort me past the casket to the side door of the chapel, where we will stand in a row, we three, and greet people as they file past. I look from one of the boys' faces to the other as we rise to our feet.

They've each clutched a handkerchief throughout the service, twisting it nervously in sweaty hands, using it frequently to dab at their tears, but now they are dry-eyed and serious, silent as they slide the soggy handkerchiefs into their jacket pockets. They each place a hand beneath one of my elbows and guide me out of the pew.

We pause together in front of the casket. They glance at me to see what they should do next. Behind us, I am conscious of a hundred pairs of eyes. I put my hands together, lacing my fingers tightly, and place them on the burnished wooden surface. I close my eyes again, and lean forward to rest my forehead lightly on my folded hands.

As I bend my neck, I can feel my hat slip out of the bobby pin in the back that has been holding it firmly to my head. It flops forward over my forehead, held now by only one pin, to just one small lock of hair above my right eye. I imagine how this must look, the hat—a silly little flat thing with just a hint of black tulle affixed to the front to suggest a veil—dangling by one dark curl over Bill's casket. I use one hand to flip it back onto my head, horrified to find that I must press the knuckles of the other against my mouth to stifle a giggle.

I open my eyes to slits and glance at Steve, on my left, and Greg, on my right. They fold their hands as I have done, rest their foreheads on their crossed thumbs, close their eyes. I don't know if they are praying, if they are saying their final goodbyes, or if, like me, they are counting slowly to one hundred, because one hundred seconds seems to me to be the appropriate length of time for us to maintain this position, before we straighten our backs and square our shoulders and prepare for the onslaught of condolences.

I can't pray, and I can't talk to Bill here in the front of the funeral home chapel, knowing that all those people are behind me, lining up now in the wide center aisle, waiting for their turn to bow their heads over his casket and pray, or say goodbye, or count to one hundred.

This is his funeral; it's the time and the place where, tradition-ally, prayers are prayed and goodbyes are said. But the setting doesn't matter to me—anyway, I know I'll be talking to him for the rest of my life, and I've already learned that sometimes, when I most need a reply from him, or when I least expect one, it will come. There's no need to say goodbye now.

And as for prayers—well, I used to think I was fairly good at praying. I usually remembered to say, in my head, little prayers of thanks for small comforts and unexpected good fortune. I seldom asked for things for myself, only for others—for Leslie's strep throat to clear up in time for her birthday party, for the pain in Grammy's hip to ease. I was never formal about my prayers, sel-dom praying at particular times or in certain places—at bedtime, or during services at church—but I would have said that I had a close, if somewhat casual, relationship with God.

That all changed on Monday night. When Reverend McCorison came to the house and stood beside me, there in the room where Bill's empty body still lay on our bed, and prayed, it was all I could do not to tell him it was of no use. Whatever he might think, what-ever his training as a minister had taught him, I knew that God wasn't there in that room with us. It wasn't a question of faith, of no longer believing. It was, rather, a conclusive knowledge that, at least at this moment, on this night, in this room, God was simply absent.

I don't know if I'll ever learn to pray again, but for now, it seems, I've given it up in favor of talking to Bill, and wishing on shooting stars.

"I never really accepted the fact that he had died"

Steve, Greg, Andy, Leslie

Steve: In the days following Dad's death, Mom found partial rolls of Tums in various of his pants pockets. She confided in me that she was sure he was having chest pain for a couple of weeks and thought it would go away.

Several of Dad's friends came down from Maine for the funeral. Mom sold Dad's '53 Chevy coupe to Sayward Lamb, and he either came to the funeral or came and picked it up soon after. Those Maine boys really dug "rust-free southern cars"!

Greg: The funeral was at night. Afterward, I stood there, with Steve, I think, not knowing what the f--- I was supposed to do as a lot of people walked by.

Of course, they had hustled Dad's body out the night he died, and the funeral was closed casket, so I got to fantasize about him being a spy in some foreign land, to return someday.

Andy: It happened so fast and out of sight. Suddenly he was gone while we were all away from home that evening.

Death was not something I thought much about before then. I had not been to a funeral before, had no idea what to expect, but in the pit of my stomach I knew I did not want to go to Dad's funeral. It was too final; I was in denial and quiet distress, not able to admit his death.

I relied on what is now called "magical thinking." If seeing is believing and you didn't see something, you didn't have to believe it. Even though he was gone and I knew he had died, somehow I felt he had not left me. (Of course it took many years to articulate this to myself.) My eleven-year-old self could not let him go.

Leslie: I was sure Dad would return someday, too. I think, because I never saw him after he left for his meeting in New York, that I never really accepted the fact that he had died. I remember dreaming—and I don't usually remember my dreams—that he was just away, and he would be coming back. Or maybe I wasn't dreaming, just fantasizing...

June 18, 1958, Westfield, New Jersey

Ruth

AFTER THE SERVICE, STEVE, GREG, AND I form a short, brave line at the side door of the chapel, and everyone begins to file slowly past us, after stopping beside the casket to pay their respects.

I am thinking about that phrase—"pay their respects"—and how it sounds as if the men should be drawing wallets from their pockets, the women fumbling among the tissues and lipsticks and compacts of pressed powder in their handbags to produce change purses that snap open with a subdued click.

Each face, as it comes closer, hovers for a moment, a foot or so from mine, before disappearing over my shoulder as I am pulled into one hug after another, some brief, some prolonged. The lapel of my good linen suit is damp with the tears of so many people, yet I can't even focus on their faces to see who they are.

After a few minutes I glance up to see Betty approaching, Elmer looming behind her. Betty is a tall woman, at least my height, but Elmer, at nearly six and a half feet, towers over her, his ruddy face and thinning carrot-colored hair bobbing above the heads of the people in front of them.

At least four people are in line between us, but as soon as I catch her eye, I think that if I have to wait another moment to fall into Betty's arms, I'll crumple to the floor on the spot. My legs, which until now have served me well, carrying me into the church and up the aisle, holding me up as we sang the closing hymn, now threaten to buckle.

With my eyes, I send Betty an urgent message, just before my vision blurs and I think to myself with a flicker of annoyance that, breakfast or no breakfast, broth or no broth, I'm going to pass out after all.

My back is pressed against the wall beside the door. Just as I feel myself start to slide down it toward the floor, I am wrapped in a pair of arms like iron bands that haul me upward and my face is pressed against a shoulder, rough in a tweed suit jacket.

I couldn't have told you what perfume Betty favored, or what brand of soap she used, but I inhale and instantly recognize her scent. Even before I hear her voice, before she pulls back a few inches and I see her eyes, I know she has cut the line to save me. I close my eyes, breathe deeply, and feel my knees stop shaking.

For long moments, I cling to her, and in a whisper too soft to be heard by anyone else, she murmurs, "I'm here, I'm here. Let's just get through this now. I won't let you fall."

When she lets go of me, she wedges herself between my back and the wall, where I can feel her warm, sturdy bulk behind me, and stays there until the pews have emptied and everyone has offered condolences and passed through the door and down the stairs. The smell of fresh coffee wafts up from the basement gathering room, and I hear the clatter of dishes as people help themselves to the plates of tea sandwiches and nut bread and lemon bars I know are spread over the long tables.

Besides Betty, the boys, and me, only Elmer and Reverend McCorison are left in the chapel. Elmer has hung back, waiting to approach me until everyone else is gone. I hear him honk loudly into his handkerchief and am surprised to see that he is crying hard, his nose and eyes red and swollen.

Dear, funny Elmer—the sober insurance man, who usually shows little emotion, but loves a good pun, and lights up like a schoolboy when he shows off his model trains—is awash in sorrow, his face wet and shiny with tears. I feel my own eyes welling, then hot tracks down my cheeks. Betty presses a dry tissue into my hand.

Sandwiched between these dearest of friends, with their hands again resting on my shoulders and the boys descending ahead of us, I sleepwalk down the stairs.

Best Friends
Amy

MY MOTHER AND ELIZABETH SWEETSER BAXTER met in the Hartford suburb of Newington, Connecticut in the mid-1940s, as young wives and mothers. Both were Maine girls—quick-witted, practical, and capable—and both were college graduates with degrees in English and a passionate love of words. Introduced by mutual friends, they became immediate allies and confidantes.

In 1947, my parents moved from their tiny starter home on Camp Avenue, where they had begun their married lives in the spring of 1942, into a rambling house at 750 Main Street. When the house directly across the street from theirs came up for sale, they couldn't wait to tell Betty and Elmer about it.

For nearly a decade the Wights and Baxters lived across Main Street from each other in Newington, and from the stories my mother told about those days, it seemed to me as if the two families had raised their collective seven children—Betty and Elmer's three boys and my own parents' three boys and one girl (I didn't come along until much later)—as one big brood.

Exiled Mainers all, these four suburban Connecticut parents encouraged their offspring in such rugged pursuits as camping, hiking, and trapping muskrats. Their children were given knives, arrows, and even rifles with which to amuse themselves. It may be that the kids spent so much time together because no one else in the neighborhood was allowed to play with them and their dangerous toys.

After my parents bought their lot on North Pond and began building our family camp, the Baxters visited them there every summer. When, later, Elmer and Betty purchased a cottage in Cumberland Foreside, close to where Betty had grown up, my family joined them there for oceanside visits.

In 1955, my father's new job with Cooper Alloy took his family away from Newington, to Westfield, New Jersey, a nearly three-hour drive to the south, bringing an end to daily visits, but not to the close friendship between the families.

Three years earlier, my dad had built a picnic table in their yard in Newington, and before they moved, Elmer helped him carry it across the street to the Baxters' backyard, where it stayed for more than fifty years, withstanding time, weather, and innumerable Baxter family gatherings.

After Elmer's retirement, he and Betty fulfilled their lifelong dream of moving back to Maine, but kept the family home in Newington. Shortly before Betty died in 2010, her oldest son's wife, Nancy, wrote to my siblings and me to say that she and Led had purchased the Connecticut house and planned to make it their retirement home. The picnic table, she said, was still there in the backyard. Would any of us like to have it back?

Andy, who lives in nearby Branford, drove to pick the table up and installed it in his yard, where it saw many more years of service.

Betty, Nancy said, "was delighted that the table will be with your family. Her words were something like, 'Good, that's where it belongs.'"

After our father died suddenly while the family was living in New Jersey, and after I was born, eight months later, the family moved back to Connecticut. We now lived in Milford, about an hour away from the Baxters, and visited frequently. As my siblings grew older and left home for college, it was usually just my mother and me who made the trip, often on Sunday afternoons after church.

Elmer and Betty's house was a wonderful place to visit, because it held so many quirks and treasures. A third-floor attic where the three boys had slept while growing up, with a system of buzzers so that Betty, in the kitchen, could communicate, using a special code, "Dinnertime!"—three short buzzes—or "Time to get up for school!"—one long, two short. A lush, terraced vegetable garden in the backyard, at the bottom of which was the scummiest, most brilliantly green frog pond. A dug-out doghouse cave in one of the garden's terraced hills where Ben's German shepherd, Phantom, slept at night to keep varmints away from Elmer's vegetables. A tiny dining room that quite comfortably contained—by some trick of spatial geometry—an enormous table, an enormous sideboard, and an enormous upright piano. An upstairs room devoted entirely to Elmer's model trains. A big black-and-white tomcat named Tim. A kitchen drawer full of shoestrings and wooden beads, paper and colored pencils, and tin soldiers. And a startling number of clocks that dinged or bonged or cuckoo-ed every hour.

I spent the afternoons exploring the nooks and crannies and marvels of the Baxters' house and yard, while my mother and Betty, with so much catching up to do, would be content to do nothing at all but talk.

On my second day of second grade, I met Donna, who instantly became my best friend in all the world, and has remained so for nearly sixty years. We spent all day together at school, and as soon as the bus dropped us off and we had checked in at home, we got together at either her house or mine for the rest of the afternoon. If for some reason we weren't together, we were on the phone with each other.

Not realizing how rare it was to be as fortunate, as well-loved, and as perfectly understood as Donna and I have always been by each other, I assumed that everyone must have a best friend. I asked my mother, who worked and cooked and cleaned and went to meetings, but never seemed to have much time to spend with friends, who her best friend was.

"Auntie Bet, of course," she answered without hesitation.

"You don't see her very much," I mused, thinking of all the hours that Donna and I spent together.

"No," she said. "But when you've been friends for as long as we have, that doesn't matter."

During the six years between my mother's death and Betty's, Betty and I wrote occasional letters to each other.

"I do miss your mother!" she wrote in one. "So often we shared thoughts without even speaking."

The last time I saw Betty was in December of 2009, just a few months before she died. Steve, Leslie, and I stopped to visit her and Elmer in the retirement home in Bar Harbor where they lived.

They treated us to lunch in the dining room and we spent a bittersweet afternoon reminiscing, all of us knowing, I think, that it would be our last visit with Betty. I brought them a tin of Christmas cookies, and she said, "These are all the kinds your mother used to make!"

Betty was no-nonsense, outdoorsy, and strong. She was smart, creative, and well-educated, a college graduate at a time when few women were. She was a historian, and as a writer she was an inspiration to me—she researched the history of Newington and turned it into an actual book you could hold in your hands. She was a formidable bridge, cribbage, and Scrabble player. She was a mom, and a surrogate mom—with three sons but no daughters, she liked to borrow Leslie and me now and then.

And she was our mother's very best friend for sixty years.

On the day Betty died, with her family by her side and Ben's wife, Joan, a nurse, in attendance, Nancy wrote to us, "Elmer was holding her hand and Joan said she actually heard her laughing and conversing with someone earlier this morning. If she was laughing with anyone, it would have been your mom."

June 20–21, 1958, Bethel, Maine

Ruth

THE FEELING OF SLEEPWALKING THROUGH my life continues throughout the next days. On Thursday morning, we say a long and difficult goodbye to Grammy, Kaye, and John. Later in the day, with Leslie, tearful but brave, once again installed at the Sweets' house, I ride, seated behind my father in the backseat of my own station wagon, with Steve in the middle and Leota behind Don, to Newington. Betty delivers Greg and Andy to Don's, and once again she hugs me tightly, until we have soaked each other's shoulders with our tears.

We drive, with Don at the wheel and the boys in the backseat, so subdued they barely speak during the whole trip, to Bethel on Friday and back to Westfield on Saturday, arriving home just before dark. In between, we bury Bill, but about this I can remember little, except how green the cemetery seems, the trees and the grass, and even the moss creeping over the shadiest spots between the graves.

In New Jersey, spring has passed and summer has begun to fade the early emerald color of the maples, the lawns already drying in the relentless heat, the blooms of the azaleas, rhododendrons, and lilacs all long past. But in Maine, where the last stubborn piles of snow have been gone for only six weeks or so, trees and bushes are flowering, and the thick new grass, lush and wet from the heavy mist that is almost, but not quite, a light rain, stains the soles of our shoes.

Bill's aunts, Lena's four sisters, are there, all sobbing quietly into their lace-edged handkerchiefs, and some of his cousins. My baby brother Gib has come from Bangor, and will drive our father home after the burial. Standing in the cemetery, he looks angry, kicks the dirt at his feet, and glares. "It's no goddamned fair," is all he says when he embraces me stiffly, and I realize how young he still is at twenty-eight, and how much he, too, loved Bill, who, since

Gib's early adolescence, has been equal parts hero and mentor to him.

After the service at the graveside, when the casket has been lowered into the ground, the boys and I walk down the hill to Don's car. Behind me, I hear a series of muffled thuds, and I know the sexton has removed the sheet of canvas from the mound of dirt beside the open grave and begun to throw the first shovelfuls onto the hardwood lid of the casket.

We stayed with Grace and Ernest at their house in town last night, and we go back there from the cemetery. The boys would have liked to stay at camp instead, but Grace wouldn't hear of it, and I knew she was right when she said there would be too much for us to do there on this quick trip. The water line hasn't been put in yet, of course, and the place has been closed up for more than nine months, since we left it, Bill padlocking the heavy home-made door for the last time, to return to New Jersey at the end of last summer.

At Grace's house, we are met by more of Bill's cousins and a raft of their young offspring. There are platters of sandwiches and cookies and cake on the long side porch, and Grace has borrowed lawn chairs from the neighbors and set them up in the yard beyond the wooden steps.

But now the rain, just a half-hearted drizzle throughout the burial service, begins to come down harder. The porch is covered but not screened, and in the still, damp air, swarms of mosquitoes seem to come from out of nowhere when we gather there. So the food is moved indoors, to the big dining room table, and the children are all given plates to fill, then shooed out to the barn, told to play there but not to get into trouble, not to step on rusty nails or fall out of the hayloft.

I'm not hungry, and I don't take a plate, but I stand beside the table holding a cut-glass punch cup in one hand. My purse, with its ready supply of tissues, dangles from the crook of my arm. The cousins and their husbands and wives come up to me one by one. I don't try to remember all their names, but just let them hug me, and give them brief one-armed hugs in return, being careful not to spill the punch on Grace's braided rug. They pat my shoulders and hands and tell me how sorry they are.

I worry about the boys, out in the barn, not because I think they'll step on a nail or fall from the hayloft, but because I know they will be ill at ease in the midst of a gang of their second cousins, most of whom have grown up together and know each other well. I picture them leaning awkwardly against the doors of the old horse stalls, talking only among themselves, or not talking at all, chewing and swallowing the sandwiches and cake they have no appetite for, wishing, as I am, for this to be over.

After a while, my legs begin to feel shaky, so I go and sit down in a rocker near one of the front windows. I tuck my purse beside me on the seat and place my hands on the wooden arms of the chair, thinking just to rest them there, but before I know it, I am clutching them tightly, as if they are handrails on a ship that is rolling and pitching on rough seas.

Bucky's wife Norma brings a cup of coffee and a plate on which she has put a triangle of tuna sandwich and a molasses cookie, and sets them on a small table beside my chair. I take a tiny sip of the coffee, but she's put cream and sugar in it, and I'm so used to drinking it black that it tastes cloyingly sweet and feels thick at the back of my throat.

When Bill and I first met, we both drank our coffee with sugar and cream. When rationing began, a month after we were married, our coupons entitled us to just a pound of sugar a week between us. It was enough for coffee, but without enough left over for much of anything else. Once the kids started to arrive, I counted up the teaspoonfuls and figured out that if we gave up sugar in our coffee, we could save enough every week for a batch of cookies, so that's what we did. Cream and canned milk were rationed by then, too, so we just switched to drinking it black. It seemed bitter at first, but we never looked back, and now I can't drink it any other way.

I pick up the cookie and nibble at the edge, but the sea-smell of the tuna suddenly overpowers me, and I have to press the back of my hand to my mouth and swallow hard to keep the bile from rising in my throat. My heart races and I feel suddenly faint.

Norma bends over me, full of concern. She has never been slim, and now, pregnant with their third child, she is stouter than ever. She is more than ten years younger than I am, only twenty-seven, but her face is round and motherly, and her eyes are warm, with smile lines crinkling the corners.

"You need some air, Ruth." She grasps my arm firmly with both her hands and pulls, helping me from the chair, and leads me out the side door from the kitchen. "And a few minutes to collect yourself, I imagine."

She settles me into another rocker on the porch, and once again I find myself gripping its wooden arms. When I realize that I am hidden from the house, tucked into the corner made by the ell that leads to the barn, I relax a little. The rain has stopped. It's still overcast, but the air feels slightly less moisture-laden and heavy, and a bit of a breeze has picked up. The mosquitoes are not too bad.

Norma peers at me. "What you need is a cold Coke," she announces, and before I know what she's about, she has called her son, eight-year-old John, from the barn. "You run over to the station and get Ruth a Coca-Cola from the machine," she tells him, pressing a nickel into his hand.

"Can I get me one, too? I only had the one today."

"Not unless you've got your own nickel."

John scowls, but he does as he's told, heading up the street toward his father's gas station, just out of sight of his grandmother's house.

Norma turns back to me. "Those kids of mine, they'd both drink Coca-Cola for breakfast, lunch, and dinner if I'd let them."

Bill and I have never let our kids drink Coke, except on special occasions, like a neighborhood barbecue or a birthday party. It costs too much for those empty calories, when they should be drinking milk and getting calcium and protein. I don't say this to Norma, of course.

Instead, I say, "I don't know what came over me just then. I'm sure I'll be fine in a minute."

"You just sit out here a few minutes, have a Coke. You'll feel better."

John is back with the Coke, ice cold, in no time. Norma pries off the cap with the church key that hangs by a string beside the porch door, and uses her thumb to flick it expertly into an old milk can in the corner, which is already half full of beer and soda bottle caps.

When she hands it to me, I think that I will take a few polite sips, and pour the rest into the hostas beside the porch steps when she's not looking. But the first swallow is so perfect—sharp, sweet, and cold—that I want to tip the heavy glass bottle up and drink it all down at once. I can't think of the last time I drank a Coke, but Norma is right; it's just what I needed.

It's not a particularly hot day, only warm and muggy, but I can tell that my face is flushed. There are tiny pinpricks of heat across my forehead, as though the skin there is stretched too tightly. I hold the cold, smooth glass against my cheek and feel little rivulets of icy condensation run down my neck and inside the collar of my dress.

Norma settles heavily into the rocker next to mine, sighing contentedly as she slips off her shoes and rests her swollen, stockinged feet on the railing of the porch.

"God, it feels awful good to take a load off," she says, and then we are both quiet for a long time, rocking slowly, as I drink my Coke.

Don drives us back to Westfield and picks up his own car on Saturday evening, and I send Greg down the street to the Sweets' house to collect Leslie. When she walks through the door, she throws herself into my arms, clings to me, and cries. I sit down in the black Boston rocker in the living room and hold her in my lap as if she were a baby, rubbing her back as we rock, saying, over and over, "There, there. There, there."

But soon there is dinner to think about, and a mountain of laundry to be done, so that the boys can pack for their Scout camping trip. Leslie can't let me out of her sight. I'm nearly tripping over her, so I give her small jobs to do, setting the table and measuring ingredients for biscuits. Later, when we've finished dinner and the dishes, I dump a basket of clean socks on the table and set her to sorting and matching them into pairs.

This has been Lena's job since she came to live with us, and after a while Leslie looks up, her dark eyes serious, and says, "I miss Grammy. She always knew just which socks were Steve's and Greg's and Andy's. They all look alike to me."

I start to tell her that they *are* all alike, that I buy dozens of pairs at a time of sturdy, nondescript socks, in black, brown, and white, and just divide them up among the three boys. Pretending to figure out which socks were whose was just a game her grandmother played with her as they folded the laundry together.

But I stop, because now she is holding up a pair of Bill's dress socks, and I see that she is crying again, sobbing so hard she can barely get the words out.

"Oh, Mommy—what will we do with Daddy's socks?"

1955, North Pond, Woodstock, Maine

Ruth

THAT NIGHT, AFTER JACK, WITH Darrell clinging to the back of his seat, had driven the bulldozer back out the road, and after our dinner of hamburgers, cooked over the campfire in a long-handled grilling basket, and marshmallows, which we toasted on the ends of slender striped maple saplings the boys cut and peeled with Bill's jackknife, we all turned in early, just after the sun had set, and before the darkness was complete. The next day, Tuesday, Bill would be making the long drive back to New Jersey.

He would depart after lunch, leaving the boys with instructions for projects enough to take them through the three days before he would turn the car around and head north once again, this time for the Fourth of July long weekend. After that, his weekends would be only two days long, and he would make the sixteen-hour round-trip every week throughout that summer—five days in New Jersey, two days in Maine—until his two weeks of vacation at the end of August. By then, he hoped, the roof would be on, the walls studded, everything ready to be closed in by Labor Day weekend, when we would all have to leave for the fall.

But first, he would set the boys to filling the craters where the stumps had been, and smoothing and leveling the spot Jack had roughed out for the camp with his dozer blade. They would lay out the footprint with string in the morning, and he would mark the places where he wanted them to dig holes for the concrete footings they would pour the following weekend.

The kids were all tired—long days in the fresh air gave them hearty appetites and put them to sleep as soon as their heads hit their pillows most nights. No one complained about the wood and canvas military cots we slept on, or the water that dripped into the tent when it rained. Even the dog, drunk on the freedom of going without collar or leash, wading into the lake whenever he pleased, digging holes in the soft forest duff and chasing squirrels up trees,

settled down beneath Bill's cot to gnaw the pine pitch from between the pads of his feet, and was soon asleep.

I lay awake, though, listening to the sounds around me. Inside
the tent, there were the regular breathing of Bill and the boys, and
Leslie's raspy wheeze as she slept on her back, louder even than
the dog's snoring. She would need her adenoids removed eventually; I was sure of it.

Outside, a snap from the direction of the campfire, which, although the boys had doused it with a bucket of lake water, still
sent up an occasional flicker of flame or small shower of sparks.
The almost inaudible lapping of tiny waves—just ripples, really—
against the shore, and the muffled sound of a light breeze moving
among the hemlock branches high overhead. That was all.

I turned onto my side, being careful not to touch the wall of the
tent beside my cot. It wasn't raining, and no rain was in the fore-
cast, but I was training myself. As long as you didn't touch the
canvas from the inside when it rained, the tent was leak-proof,
mostly, except for those few spots in the seam between the wall
and ceiling where the canvas had worn thin. Touch the inside of
it, though, and water would immediately start coming through the
canvas where you had brushed it, or bumped it, or pushed your
cot up against it. The boys knew this well from their Scout trips,
and had lectured Leslie about it until they were satisfied she
wouldn't try it just to see what would happen.

I lay thinking about what it would be like the next night, settling down to sleep in the tent without Bill. It would be far from
the first time I had been on my own with the four kids—Bill had
taken occasional overnight business trips, and, of course, he'd already been working in New Jersey for three weeks before we drove
to Maine on Saturday. It wouldn't even be the first night I had
spent camping with the kids and without their father. Only the
summer before, when the Wight and Baxter families camped together at a park an hour from home, Betty and I had stayed on
through the week with the kids while Elmer and Bill returned to
Newington to go to work.

But that was a campground, with sites placed close enough together to hear a baby cry or a father belch inside the tent at the
next campsite. It had a campground store that sold overpriced
milk and bread and eggs and twenty-one flavors of hard candy

sticks, and even a little playground with swings and a rusty slide, where I could send Leslie with one or two of the boys to watch her if Betty and I wanted a little peace and quiet in the mid-afternoon. Here, a mile from the paved road, on the quiet side of this quiet lake, the kids and I would be more alone than ever before once Bill left.

Sometime later, an hour or maybe two, still unable to sleep, I sighed and got up quietly, trying not to wake the others, to make my way to the outhouse.

We'd thrown the rudimentary structure up hastily that weekend, over a pit the boys had dug. We'd built it out of two-by-fours and sheathed the walls with old green shutters Bill had found in the hayloft of his aunt's barn in Bethel. I had built the "toilet" myself, a two-level wooden box with two oval holes cut in the top and square wooden covers hinged with scraps of leather.

"A two-seater!" I told the kids proudly. Half of it was at a more or less standard height, and half was low enough for Leslie to use without assistance, once I had reassured her that she wouldn't fall down the hole. I had added a shelf with room for a can of lime, a roll of toilet paper, and a stack of magazines—"all the comforts of home," I bragged.

Now, tucking a flashlight into the pocket of my pajama bottoms, I untied the four pairs of canvas strips that kept the tent flaps closed and slipped out, retying the flaps behind me to keep out the voracious mosquitoes that swarmed each evening, as soon as we let the smoke from the campfire die down.

When I turned and straightened, I drew in my breath sharply. A half moon was just about to dip behind the small mountain to the west, across the lake. Its light was moving on the surface of the water, dancing like fireflies over the ripples, but it wasn't that light that made me gasp.

Here and there on the ground, in every hole where a stump had stood, each chopped-off root was alight with green fire. Thirty yards from the tent, at the edge of the woods, patches of green light shone from the pile of stumps Jack had dumped there.

Transfixed, I walked slowly toward the glow. Drawing near and bending down, I could see that it came from minute fungi clustered along the roots. Forgetting about the outhouse, I moved from one luminous crater to the next. When I switched off my flashlight, the green fire intensified. As I watched, the moon slipped behind the mountain, and then the only light was the unearthly green glow at my feet.

"Bill!" My voice came out in a croak. "Wake up! Kids—come outside! Hurry! I don't know how long it will last!"

There was a rustling and muttering inside the tent. "What? What?" Bill stood and switched on the big green battery-powered lantern, and shadows sprang to life on the canvas walls. I could see the outlines of the three boys, instantly alert, already swinging their legs from their cots, and Leslie, sitting up more slowly, stretching her arms over her head.

"Is it morning?" she asked sleepily.

I stuck my head back in through the tent flaps. "No, it's the middle of the night, but wait till you see—hurry! I don't want you to miss it!"

"Is it a bear?"

"No, it's not a bear."

"Is it a moose?"

"No, it's not a moose. Hurry!"

Leslie was rummaging under her pillow. "I can't find my flashlight."

"You won't need it. Come on, you'll see."

Bill and the kids stumbled from the tent, then stopped short.

"There!" I said triumphantly. "Have you ever in your life *heard* of such a thing?"

"Foxfire," said Bill, awed. "It comes from a fungus that lives on decaying wood. I've heard of it, but I've sure never seen it. Bioluminescence, that's the scientific name."

The boys circled the pile of stumps, peering closely at the patches of fungus, their faces glowing green in its light.

"Holy cow," one of them said, but quietly, reverently.

"Is foxfire fairy light, Daddy?" Leslie asked.

"It's coming from tiny mushrooms, see here? And here? I don't know just what it is that makes them glow."

"I think it's light for the fairies to see by."

"I think you might be right."

In the morning, there was a heavy dew over everything. When the sun came up, intricate spider webs, strung among the upended tree roots and over the leaves of the blueberry bush, shone silver and gold with fine strands of droplets.

"Fairy dresses!" Leslie exclaimed. "See, Daddy, it *was* the fairies—they needed the foxfire light to wash their dresses and spread them out to dry."

Northern Lights

Amy

One night you woke me late
And said, Come see
The Northern Lights.
I feigned sleep;
I was so snug—
and smug. But then I thought,
Why not? And I came barefoot
Down the narrow stairs.
We pushed the canoe off—
Skritch—over the sand.
The hem of my nightgown brushed the water
As I climbed into the bow.
(You were in charge:
You took the stern.)
The lake was black.
The trees were black.
The sky was black,
Pricked with stars—
No moon.
Our paddles dipped, and dripped,
Not silent as the Indians', but hushed
Enough to hear the bats
And the crackle of someone's campfire
Down the lake.
And they were there, in the northwest sky—
Green, yellow, and red
(Just like Robert Service said).

June 23–27, 1958, Westfield, New Jersey
Ruth

IT SEEMS STRANGE TO LIE IN BED on Monday morning, a week after Bill's death, and know that Leslie and I are alone in the house. The boys left yesterday after church for their Scout trip, feigning enthusiasm as they loaded their camping equipment into the back of our station wagon. I let one of the leaders, Tom Street, take my car for the week because it was big enough to haul several boys and their gear. His little sedan sits in our driveway now, the key hung on a hook by the back door, but I don't intend to drive it. There's nowhere I need to go, not with the freezer still full of the casseroles our neighbors brought last week and now, far too much milk on hand. I've forgotten to let the dairy know the boys will be gone this week, and the milk truck—that's what woke me just now, I realize—has just left our usual order in the galvanized metal box beside the back steps.

At the supper table on Saturday evening, after we'd returned from Bethel, Andy pointed out, tentatively, that if they hadn't had the Scout trip planned, we could have gone back to Maine for the summer a week sooner. I knew they must all be dreading the days ahead—packed into a damp tent with several other boys who wouldn't know what to say to them, and so would probably say little or nothing, and being asked over and over by the adults if there was anything they could do to help—and I was tempted, for just a moment, to tell them they didn't have to go.

But—"They've made a commitment, Ruth," said Bill's voice inside my head. "They need to honor it."

Before I had a chance to relay this to the boys, the words I intended to say—Bill's words—came instead from Steve's mouth. He laid his fork down and sat up straight in his chair before he started to speak.

"We have to honor our commitment. You guys know that."

His brothers nodded. Of course.

"Besides," he added, "with everything Dad taught us when we built the camp, we probably know more about clearing brush and carpentering than anyone else who's going. They're going to need us."

And so they left yesterday at eleven-thirty, taking peanut butter sandwiches to eat on the way, and a double batch of fresh brownies, wrapped in waxed paper and tucked in with their gear, to share with their fellow Scouts.

It was Bill's birthday yesterday, or would have been. His forty-sixth. I hadn't said a word, but I knew the kids were all thinking about it at breakfast, remembering my tradition of putting a birthday candle in a muffin or a stack of pancakes on every family birthday, to start the celebration early.

At church, I'd turned down an invitation to have Sunday dinner with the Sweets, saying I had things I needed to get done. I'd told Leslie she could go, and play with Diana for the afternoon, but she shook her head fiercely and clung to my side.

"*No,* Mommy!" she whispered. "I want to stay with you!"

So we ate our own sandwiches on the back porch, then I read a magazine while Leslie, without being asked, got out the dog's brush and began to groom his silky fur.

"Lucky likes me to brush him best, so it can be my job from now on, Mommy."

"That's nice," I answered, leafing absently through the *Ladies' Home Journal.*

"I can walk him and feed him, too."

"That will be a big help."

"The boys won't have time anymore."

"No?"

"No, Mommy, because they have to do all Daddy's jobs from now on."

Now she breathes evenly beside me in the early morning light, her tousled head on Bill's pillow. I've given up, for now, trying to get her to sleep in her own bed. At least when she sleeps with me, I can soothe her as soon as she stirs, whimpering softly, in the night, instead of waiting until she stumbles, wailing and fully awake, into my room, needing a drink of water, a backrub, and endless lullabies before she can fall back to sleep.

It's still dark, but the glowing hands of the clock on the bedside table tell me the time: 4:50. Too early for me to get up, but too late to get back to sleep, I know. The sun hasn't yet risen, but through the window I can see that the sky has begun to lighten. I lie on my back and stare up at the smooth white ceiling.

A week ago I awoke in this bed with Bill beside me, another work week about to start for him. The day trip into New York City lay ahead of him on that other Monday morning, the one that feels so long ago now.

And in just one more week, when I wake in the morning, I'll look up to see the familiar knots in the pine boards of the bedroom ceiling at camp. Bill and I used to lie on our backs there together, watching as the gradual lightening of dawn revealed the group of knots on one board, directly over our bed, that resembles a pork chop and two fried eggs, and the one, near the closet, that looks just like an impish pixy face.

On Tuesday evening, when I pick up the ringing phone, I am surprised to hear the voice of Sayward Lamb, our camp neighbor. There's static on the line for the long-distance call from Maine, but even so, I can tell he's choking up when he tells me how sorry they are, he and Cynthia, for my loss.

"Thank you," I say, and add that it's nice of him to call. I don't know them that well, really, but he and Bill were friendly, and helped each other out now and then with projects at our respective camps.

He clears his throat then and says he's wondering about Bill's car. Do I plan to keep it? Because if not, he says, he'd like to buy it from me. "For a fair price," he hastens to add, and names a figure that's more than I think it's worth. He doesn't want me to feel pressured; it's only that he thought I might be wanting to sell it.

The 1953 Chevy sedan, the car Bill bought the summer he started his job in New Jersey, is still in good shape. I do want to sell it, of course—I can't drive two cars, and Steve is not even fifteen yet, more than a year away from getting a license.

The big Chevy station wagon that I drive now is a 1956, bought new to replace the high-mileage former salesman's car I drove for a year or two. The first brand new car we'd ever had, it still feels

practically new to me, and when we head for Maine for the summer, we'll need every inch of its roomy interior, so of course that's
the car we'll keep.

Bill's car is another one of those things, I realize, to which I
haven't given much thought. If Sayward buys it, it will be a weight
off my shoulders, and he is clearly pleased by the idea of buying a
car that has never been through a Maine winter. He says, quickly,
that someone he knows is coming down our way on Friday, and
he can get a ride down and pick it up then. If I'm sure.

I wonder if it will be hard for the kids to see it parked there at
Sayward and Cynthia's camp, each time we drive past this summer on the way to and from ours. I wonder if it will be hard for
me. But I dismiss the thought—after all, it's only a car. I tell him
I'm sure.

1955–1956, Westfield, New Jersey

Ruth

LEAVING MAINE AND OUR LOT ON North Pond at summer's end was harder than I had imagined, partly because we hadn't made as much progress on the camp as Bill had hoped. I knew he wished we could have spent a few more of the perfect late-summer days working on it, especially now that the boys had become so proficient with hammers and saws. Instead, in late August he hired a local carpenter, Jim Spinney, with instructions to finish installing the siding, windows, and doors to keep out the weather.

Steve would be starting seventh grade, and classes at the junior high in Westfield were to begin on the Thursday before Labor Day; the elementary school would start a week later. So when Bill left for New Jersey after lunch on the last Sunday in August, Steve went with him, leaving the younger kids and me to make the most of our last few days at the lake before we headed back to Newington to finish up the packing I'd begun back in June.

It felt like a leap of faith, loading up the car on Friday morning and driving out the road, leaving a stranger in charge of the place that, only half-built, had already come to mean so much to each of us.

And it wasn't just that. All summer I'd succeeded in putting out of my mind what I now had to face squarely: in just a few days, I'd watch our belongings being loaded into a moving van for the trip to Westfield, to the new house on Fairfield Circle, where none of us knew a soul, where the kids would all be starting school in a new place.

The summer had made me feel competent and self-assured, almost brash, but as I drove south, my confidence evaporated. Camping in the woods for weeks on end with four children, splitting kindling for a campfire, binding up a sprained ankle—those things now seemed easy. But meeting new neighbors, joining a new church, finding my way around a new town twice the size of Newington—those were the things that caused a knot in the pit of my stomach as the miles ticked by. I wished I could fast-forward to next June, point the car north, and become once again that capable, composed version of myself.

Despite my fears, the move went smoothly. Bill had attended the closing for our new house in Westfield that Friday afternoon, and he and Steve drove up to Newington after school. They had already arrived at what I now forced myself to think of as our "old house" when we pulled into the driveway shortly before dusk.

On Monday morning, Betty and Elmer and the boys came over. Elmer and Bill picked up the sturdy wooden picnic table Bill had built a few years earlier, carried it across the street, and set it beneath the apple tree in the Baxters' backyard. I tried not to cry.

We all stood together on our front steps for the last time, and watched as the high school band led the Labor Day parade down Main Street. Then we crossed the street. Betty brought out a red-checked tablecloth, potato salad, hot dogs, potato chips, brownies, and we all squeezed onto the two long benches. Betty and I sat opposite each other. We tried not to cry.

Bill and Steve left for Westfield in the late afternoon; the rest of us would follow the moving van the next morning. The packing was done. That night, after Betty brought over sandwiches for our supper and muffins for us to have for breakfast, Andy and Greg bedded down on a mattress on the floor of their old bedroom. Leslie shared another with me on the floor of the room at the top of the stairs that had been Bill's and mine. Very soon her raspy breathing became regular, the only sound I could hear from within the house, now that the mantel clock had been allowed to run down and was packed into one of the stack of boxes marked "Living Room." I cried myself to sleep.

By mid-fall we were settling into our new house, new neighborhood, new town. The kids were doing well in school and beginning to make friends. Our suburban street, with its dozens of young families, was ready-made for making new friends, both for the kids and for me.

Most mornings, once they had sent their kids off to school, washed the breakfast dishes, and started the laundry, the women would gather for coffee at one or another's kitchen table, and they were quick to include me. Like the others, I brought along mending or knitting to keep my hands busy while we chatted the day away. We would call the grocery store and have what we needed for dinner delivered to whichever house we were at that morning. When the groceries arrived, that was our signal to go back to our own homes to put them away, hang out the wash, sweep the floors, and start dinner before the kids got home from school.

Though I was relieved to be accepted into this group of young mothers, and grateful for our similar circumstances—husbands who worked long hours at demanding jobs, kids in the same schools—I missed my old friends, especially Betty, and missed living close enough to Don and Leota to run over to their house anytime. We called, and wrote each other letters, and every couple of months, on a Sunday after church, Bill and I packed the kids into the station wagon and drove to Newington to spend the afternoon at either Betty and Elmer's, or Don and Leota's.

Autumn passed, and winter—our first Christmas in Westfield, Andy's ninth birthday on New Year's Eve, then, in February, my thirty-sixth. There was more snow than usual for New Jersey that year, but not more than we had been used to in Newington. In mid-March, though, when the daffodils were already in bloom, the entire Mid-Atlantic region, as well as southern New England, was slammed by three snowstorms in the span of a week and a half, including a late-winter nor'easter that brought high winds and nearly two feet of snow.

The storms began on a Wednesday and continued off and on throughout the following week. The plows couldn't keep up with the rapid accumulation of snow, and the kids' schools were closed for five days. They staged snowball fights, dug tunnels and built snow forts, and went sledding with their friends, but we all knew the missed days would have to be added to the end of the school year in June, delaying our return to the camp.

Easter, which fell early, on April first, was cold and clear. We woke the kids before dawn and made the three-hour drive to Newington, to spend the day with Elmer and Betty and their boys, and attend the Easter service at our old church. The yards along Main Street were still snow-covered, and I had to remind the kids, in their dress shoes, to stay off of the high snowbanks on our short walk to Newington Congregational.

Our old neighbors waved and called out to us, and everyone at church greeted us warmly, eager to hear about life in New Jersey. It filled my heart to bursting, being surrounded by so many dear friends. In the afternoon we dined on Betty's good china—ham with all the fixings, and chocolate cake with fluffy seven-minute frosting—then we pushed back our chairs, but stayed at the table for hours, talking and laughing together. It felt like old times, and it was only on the drive back, as I watched the brightly colored lights along the Berlin Turnpike slide by, carrying us south, that I understood that Newington was no longer my home, and I would never again be anything but a visitor to my old life.

Real spring came at last, and, close on its heels, even before the end of May, the oppressive heat and humidity of a New Jersey summer. The last weeks of school dragged, but finally it was the last Saturday in June, the cars were packed, the breakfast dishes done and put away, and we were off to Maine. Going home.

June 28, 1958, Westfield, New Jersey

Ruth

TOM STREET BRINGS THE BOYS HOME late in the afternoon on Saturday. They are tired and filthy, each of them dragging a duffel bag bulging with dirty laundry. Their arms and legs are covered with scratches and bug bites, and Andy has a blood blister under his left thumbnail, from missing a nail and hitting his thumb instead with a hammer. He shakes his head when I ask if it hurts.

"Mommy sold Daddy's car to Mr. Lamb," Leslie tells them importantly, before they have a chance to ask where it is. "He came yesterday and drove it away to Maine."

I see three sets of eyes go quickly to the empty spot in the driveway, but none of them says a word. While I help Tom transfer the troop's gear from the back of the station wagon to the trunk of his car, they climb heavily up the three steps to the side door.

It was right there, at that door, that Reverend McCorison met them twelve days ago, and said those words—"The time has come for you to become men." The words that ended their childhood, or at least ended childhood as they had known it.

Because if they are not men—these world-weary souls, shouldering their bags when they reach the door, each brother careful not to let it slam on the one behind him—they are surely no longer boys. Although, of course, "the boys" is what I will still call them—will always call them, I expect, until the day I die.

Andy—last in the line of straggling survivors, home from whatever war they have fought this past week—waits at the door, holding it open for Leslie, then for me.

For six days, they've been out of my sight, coming to terms as well as they can with the thing that none of us will ever really come to terms with, learning to live in a new kind of world, to take on a new role, in a new kind of family. They've been learning to become men.

It's all I can do not to sit down on the top step and cry for my lost boys.

Summer 1956, North Pond, Woodstock, Maine

Ruth

AFTER OUR PREVIOUS SUMMER in the tent, the camp, with its four solid walls and a roof that kept out the rain, felt luxurious. We could look out at the lake through real glass windows, even if most of them were only temporary—old wooden storm windows, fixed in place, that Bill had picked up, and which he planned to replace with double-hung windows that actually opened, as soon as we could afford it. We had screen doors, and only an occasional mosquito found its way inside at night, drawn to the glow of our real electric lights.

Under the window in what was becoming the kitchen, Bill installed the deep farmhouse sink we'd found at an auction, connected a drain to carry the graywater to a drywell he and the boys had dug, and hooked up a pitcher pump to bring water from the lake into the sink. He wired an outlet for the wide electric range we'd replaced with a new one in the house in Westfield and hauled to Maine on a trailer, and another for a small refrigerator with a freezer compartment barely big enough for a tray of ice cubes.

Cupboard doors would have to wait, but he mounted upper shelves to one wall to hold our food and dishes, and built rough wider ones below for pots and pans.

There was still so much to do. Among our priorities were walls to enclose two tiny bedrooms downstairs, and pine boards for flooring in the loft, which would then become a cozy space for the boys to sleep up under the rafters. We needed linoleum to cover the pine plank floors, curtains for the windows, overhead lights above the sink and the big oak table.

Bill worked feverishly every weekend, barely taking time to eat or even sit down. He and the boys floored the loft, using a ladder to go up and down with the lumber and tools, and then passing up the old twin bedsteads and lumpy mattresses we'd acquired over the past year. The very first night that the boys went upstairs to sleep, he began—at half past nine—to lay out the stringers for a steep, narrow staircase to replace the ladder.

"How are the kids supposed to sleep with you sawing and hammering?" I asked him, but he was determined that before he left for New Jersey the next day, there would be stairs.

And there were. I helped for an hour or so, marking boards for Bill to cut with the Skilsaw outside the door, where he had rigged up a trouble light on the overhang of the roof and set up a couple of sawhorses, but I soon gave up and went to bed myself. There had been no sound from the boys in the loft, and, somehow, even with the racket, Leslie had fallen asleep on her cot downstairs, just a few yards from the hammering. Hard work, plenty of exercise, and fresh air meant sleep came easily, and before long I had drifted off, too.

Although Bill slid into bed as quietly as he could, I woke up and looked at my watch; it was well after two in the morning. He'd be lucky to get three or four hours of sleep; then, I knew, he'd be up and tackling another project before he had to leave in mid-afternoon. He seemed to thrive on the pace he'd set for himself, but I worried he'd become run-down if he didn't take some time to relax. I knew that when he wasn't here with us, he was putting in long hours at work, getting as much done as he could in order to be able to take his two weeks of vacation later in the summer. And then there was the driving—eight hours to come north on Friday nights, eight more to get back on Sunday in time to catch a few hours of sleep before another long work week. I worried about him.

In the morning, when we heard the boys stirring in the loft, we both went to the bottom of the staircase to see their reactions when they saw the results of their father's midnight labors.

They were hesitant at first.

"They're already finished?" Greg asked incredulously. "We can use them?" He put one foot on the top step, tentatively, as if testing it.

"They're finished!" Bill said, and we watched as, one at a time, they came slowly down.

Within days, they'd be thundering up and down the stairs, grabbing onto the horizontal support beam beside them on their descent and swinging themselves out, dropping down with a thud in the middle of the living room floor.

Summer 1956

Greg

UPON OUR RETURN TO CAMP IN THE summer of 1956, someone met us with great concern about a two-by-four stud in the back wall that had split due to the load. Apparently it was fixed okay.

Dad worked morning to night at camp. He had tasked us to shore up the banking behind the camp with logs, stakes, rocks, and dirt. When he next came, our work was not enough, and he cut bigger trees and put in more substantial shoring.

We had a one-armed guy deliver sand to the top of the hill and we wheelbarrowed dozens of loads to the beach.

Our first outboard motor was a hugely heavy air-cooled Lawson six horsepower on the Casco Bay boat with the transom raised. We skinny boys could surf board behind it.

Berry-picking...shooting bottles...trips to Lee's in the boat ...Screw Auger Falls...visits to Bangor. Pull-everything-out-of-the-fridge lunches; when Dad came, he would eat peanut butter and sardine sandwiches. Homemade root beer under the sink, occasionally exploding...Lucky the cocker spaniel...rescuing the float and building a new anchor...

June 29, 1958, Westfield, New Jersey
Ruth

WE COULD HAVE WAITED AND LEFT on Monday, could have gone to church in the morning on Sunday and passed a leisurely afternoon preparing to leave for the summer in Maine. But I spent the week the boys were gone—when I wasn't writing thank-you notes for the flowers and casseroles and cards that had poured in since Bill's death, or sitting on the back porch, trying to make sense of the words that swam on the pages of a magazine—gathering most of what we'd need to bring with us and piling it next to the door in the kitchen.

Except for our clothes and the perishable food from the cupboards, it isn't really that much. The kitchen at camp is well supplied with cast-off pots, pans, dishes, and silverware. Tucked under the eaves in the loft, huge, thick cardboard drums Bill brought home from work, which once contained dry chemicals of some sort, now hold stacks of lumpy pillows, old bedspreads, and the rough woolen blankets that were a bargain at Army surplus stores in the years after the war. Sheets and pillowcases are crammed into the drawers of several old dressers, sprinkled liberally with mothballs to repel not only moths, we hope, but mice.

In the closet-like room we call a bathroom—although it holds neither a toilet nor a bathtub, only an ancient porcelain sink that has to be filled with warm water from a teakettle for washing up—a mirrored medicine cabinet is stocked with toothpaste, aspirin, and first aid supplies. The bathroom shelves hold towels and facecloths, and the bars of Ivory soap we use for bathing in the lake—because it floats, and because it is, according to the slogan, "99 and 44/100% pure," which we hope means it won't kill the fish.

We've even left an assortment of jeans, shorts, and faded t-shirts, rubber thong sandals and old canvas sneakers in the closets and dressers. We could almost get by without packing much more than a few pairs of underwear, except that we never wear our "camp clothes" to town for errands, and I know the kids will have outgrown much of what they left behind last summer.

I started in right away last night on the pile of rank laundry the boys brought home from their camping trip, using the clothes dryer instead of hanging it out to dry on the line. Six loads later, close to midnight, the last of their underwear and socks had been folded and added to the three piles on the dining room table. I tiptoed into their rooms, placing a stack on each dresser for them to pack back into their duffle bags in the morning and wedge into the back of the station wagon.

Then I fell into bed, nudging Leslie as gently as I could out of the center of the mattress, where she'd fallen asleep on her back with her arms outstretched. She stirred slightly and mumbled something, but didn't awaken.

I slept only intermittently myself, nervous about the long drive, even though the car had made the same trip just a week earlier. That time, with Don driving and all of us, I suppose, still in shock, we'd simply gotten in and ridden mindlessly north, with no thought of checking the oil, the tire pressure, or the coolant level beforehand, as Bill had always done before our trips to Maine.

Bill's cousin Bucky had changed the oil for us before we left Bethel on Saturday to return home. Without a word to me about it, he'd shown up at his parents' house early in the morning, before the burial, while Grace and I sat at the kitchen table drinking coffee, and everyone else still slept upstairs. He'd asked for the keys and driven my car over to his gas station, returning it scarcely a half-hour later.

"Tires look fine," he told me. "Oil was down some, maybe half a quart, that's all. Looked a little dirty. Probably would have been okay, but you got a long drive ahead. Figured I'd change it and you'll be good for a while."

He refused any money for the oil change, or for the gas he'd put in the tank. Grace, who had made up every spare bed in the house, put out piles of clean towels, and fed all of us since our arrival the day before, wouldn't let me lift a finger to help, nor pay for so much as a loaf of bread or a quart of milk.

"You're family," she kept saying, slipping a tissue from the sleeve of her blouse and using it to dab at the corners of her eyes.

Now I am up, as usual, at first light. I know the boys are exhausted, and I am being as quiet as I can as I start to load the station wagon, hoping they'll sleep in for a bit longer. But I've made only a couple of trips from the kitchen door to the car before all three of them materialize silently beside me in the driveway, fully dressed, ghostlike in the muted gray light, each bearing a stack of boxes or a duffel bag.

Summer 1957, North Pond, Woodstock, Maine

Ruth

OUR THIRD SUMMER ON THE POND began with a heat wave, with temperatures soaring into the mid-eighties. It was hot for June in Maine, but still more comfortable than what we left behind in New Jersey, where it had been ten degrees hotter and far muggier. The kids dragged themselves through their last school days in stagnant air thick with humidity, while, at home, I tied a kerchief around my head to keep sweat from getting into my eyes while I gathered, packed, and planned.

School was let out early on Friday. Leslie came home from her last day of second grade in the early afternoon, flung herself down on the couch and announced that the first thing she was going to do when we got to camp the next day was jump in the lake.

"Doesn't that sound wonderful? I think I'll join you," I said.

We packed both cars that evening after supper, and pulled out of the driveway the next morning after an early breakfast, the boys in the sedan with Bill, and Leslie in the front passenger seat of the station wagon with me. By midafternoon we were exiting the

Maine Turnpike in Gray and turning onto Route 26 for the last hour of the trip.

A mile north of the village of Bryant Pond, and less than a half-mile before our turn, we stopped at the roadside spring. Bill and I poured out the remainder of the gallon of Westfield tap water we'd taken in each car and refilled the empty jugs with cold, clean water from the two pipes that ran, side by side, down from the mountain.

"The best in the world," Bill said, raising the glass jug he'd just finished filling and tapping it lightly against mine in a toast.

Two years ago, during our first summer here, he'd tried digging a spring fifty yards up the hillside behind the camp and piping the water down to the road, thinking it would be more convenient to get our drinking water right there. The water was clear, and tasted fine, but it ran so slowly that it took a long time to fill even one jug, and we continued to use the roadside spring most of the time.

Since our small refrigerator was usually full to bursting with food for six people, that spring had soon been designated as a place to chill our homemade root beer, the Fourth of July water-melon, and, when Bill's friends visited, their beer.

Last summer, Pip Cummings had come, along with two or three cronies, to help Bill install shiny metal roofing over the tar-paper we'd put on the roof the first year. A Bethel boy, younger than Bill by a decade or so, Pip had married Ada Cotton, whom we called "Little Ada"; she was Ada Balentine's niece, but had been raised by her as a daughter. We knew them from the time we spent in previous summers at Big Ada's camp at the end of North Pond, but also because Pip and Little Ada had recently moved their young family to New Jersey, and they'd stayed with us while house-hunting.

Pip was there to repay his debt in labor and, apparently, beer; he brought along at least a case, maybe two. Liberal consumption began as soon as lunch was over, and soon I heard Pip telling Bill the spring he'd dug wasn't big enough to keep it all cold.

"I guess I'll have to dig it out a little more before you fellows come again," Bill said.

"Nope, nope, I've got a better idea! Got something right here that should do the trick!" Pip started for his truck.

I was inside with Leslie, clearing away the lunch dishes, when we heard the explosion, followed by the banging and rattling of rocks and clods of dirt raining down on the new metal roof. We ran outside to find Bill and Pip up on the road. Pip was waving his arms and shouting jubilantly.

"I guess to Christ that oughtta do it!" he yelled.

"Good lord!" I shouted up to Bill. "What *was* that?"

It was Greg who answered, from under the porch, where he'd taken cover. "They threw a stick of dynamite in the spring to make it bigger!" he said, clearly impressed.

From the road, Bill grinned down at me. "Now, I know what you're thinking, but don't say anything you'll regret," he called, laughing.

Taking his advice, I grabbed Leslie by the wrist and stalked back inside.

I set the jug of water on the floor at Leslie's feet and climbed back into the driver's seat to follow Bill in the camp road. We hadn't gone more than a tenth of a mile after turning off the tar when Bill stopped the car. I saw Greg push one of the back doors open; Lucky barreled out, as if shot from a cannon, and began to run down the road ahead of the car. By the time we had pulled over and parked behind the camp, he was already in the lake, reveling in the freedom he somehow remembered from the year before.

Bill had only a day to settle in before he had to turn around and make the long drive back to New Jersey, but he was back the next weekend for the first of his two vacation weeks, bringing with him Ray Nevin from next door. Ray, who was in Andy's class at school, brought along a portable record player and a stack of 45 rpm records, and for a week the peace of the pond was shattered by "Whole Lotta Shakin' Goin' On" and "Roll Over, Beethoven," played at top volume.

Besides treating us all to the rock and roll music of Jerry Lee Lewis and Chuck Berry, Ray provided the kids' first introduction to Elvis Presley, who he said was his older sister's heartthrob, and by the end of the week even seven-year-old Leslie was dancing on the porch and belting out "You ain't nothin' but a hound dog."

It made us all laugh, but I had read about Elvis—his lewd move-ments on stage, and his unsavory effect on his smitten teenage fans—and I hoped she would forget all about the song by the time we went back to Westfield at the end of the summer. I thought about how mortifying it would be if she started third grade, was assigned a composition on "What I Did Last Summer," and wrote about learning to dance and sing like Elvis.

"Time was soft there"

Andy, Leslie, Amy

Amy: When I was a kid, the trip to Maine at the end of the school year was a really big deal, with lots of memories of the trip itself—roadside picnics, stopping at Hebert's Candies (only occasionally, but it made a big impression), crossing the old green bridge into Kittery, the Sardine Man—but the clearest memories are of how it felt when we turned onto the camp road, and that moment when we finally got to camp, after waiting for ten months to be back. I remember once when we were driving in the road for the first time of the summer, and I suddenly thought, *this* is what people mean when they say, "My heart was in my throat."

Leslie: The green bridge was definitely a high point, and meant we were finally in Maine. As we approached the bridge, Dad always quoted Washington Irving: "Once you cross that bridge, my friend, the ghost is through, his power ends!" We all breathed a sigh of relief to reach that point.

The next stop on our trip was often Howard Johnson's on the traffic circle in Kittery for ice cream. I sometimes talked Dad into going around the circle a couple of times before we pulled into the HoJo's parking lot.

A stop at the spring to fill up a water jug with the coldest, most refreshing water, then on to camp!

I remember all being dressed alike in tan chino shorts. I'm sure our shirts also matched, but only the shorts stand out. Lucky would get so excited when we got close to camp, and would dig his claws into our bare legs as he scrambled across us, searching for a way out of the car to be the first to arrive at camp.

Andy: Once across the old Kittery Bridge, it always felt to me that we were *there* in the sense that all of Maine was where we wanted to be. I remember so many landmarks along Route 26 from Gray. Always looking the same year to year—a great comfort of the familiar, places where time stood still waiting for us. But turning down the camp road was a different feeling—big, pit-of-stomach excitement to be back, with a sharpened outlook to see any little signs of change: someone's new name sign, pile of gravel, pothole (some seemed to be exactly the same), fresh boards or paint, fresh cuts on a log road...

We were entering our own realm, where changes were welcomed signs of growth within the familiar and all needed careful notice. The air was different: fresher, fir-scented, delicious as that spring water.

As we rolled over that last little hill by Lambs', our rough-dug "turnaround" came into view and we were there. Dad would pull in to park on the left side of the narrow road above the camp. Thinking back, I'd swear there was a brief instant when we all took in that view before the car doors burst open and we spilled out to begin another summer. We kids all grabbed some part of the gear and rushed down the sloped path—no stairs yet in those early years. First one there would reach up for the key "hidden" on the door frame, unlock, and rush inside.

Decades later, I read a book titled *Time Was Soft There,* about a town on the Isle of Wight full of used bookstores. The unique atmosphere created by that community and its wonderfully quirky residents was a balm to all visitors. Reading that book, I found words for the memories of getting to camp. After serving "hard time" throughout the school year, at camp it felt different. Time was soft there.

July 3, 1958, Maine

Ruth

I HAVE ALMOST FORGOTTEN ABOUT the boat when I stop at Bucky's gas station in Bethel and he tells me it has arrived on the train. Leslie and I are running errands while we wait for our clothes to finish washing at the laundromat; I've allowed the boys the freedom of wandering up and down Main Street while we shop.

We've been, first, to Brown's Variety for a dish drainer, a paring knife, and two new pie plates. For the most part, I've outfitted the kitchen at camp with second-hand cookware and utensils from rummage sales and the annual Boy Scout auction in West Paris, and I'm gradually filling in a few gaps. We've gotten groceries at Bryant's IGA, including hot dogs, marshmallows, chips, and Cokes for a Fourth of July cookout tomorrow, although it will just be the five of us.

Now we've stopped to fill the car's tank before we go back to collect the laundry. Since it's a hot, breezy day, I'll hang it out to dry on the clothesline Bill strung on a pulley between the camp and a hemlock tree. Bucky is pumping our gas, washing our windshield with uncommon attention to detail, as if to avoid looking at me as I sit in the driver's seat, waiting to pay.

When he comes to the window he looks almost apologetic as he says, "That boat Bill ordered is in," as if he thinks if he didn't have to say the name, if he didn't remind me of Bill's loss, that I'd be able to forget it.

"It's over to the station." He jerks his head toward the train station, just across the street. "Aluminum boat, it ain't too heavy. I can bring it down for you this evening if you want."

I give Bucky an extra two dollars and ask if he can bring along a five-gallon can of gas and a quart of mixing oil for the outboard motor. Then I drive across to the station and park in the unpaved lot.

Leslie and I get out of the car and sure enough, in an open shed next to the station is the biggest cardboard box we've ever seen.

Leslie looks momentarily stricken when she reads Bill's name on the shipping label, but I say, with cheerful determination, "Daddy ordered this for you kids to have fun with at camp! Won't the boys be excited? Let's keep it a secret that it's come until Bucky brings it down to camp tonight."

I collect the laundry and find the boys, who are walking up Main Street, eating popsicles they've bought at the Bethel Spa, a popular diner that also carries a selection of newspapers, candy, gum, and ice cream. Before they climb into the backseat, I look at Leslie and hold my finger to my lips. She's practically jumping up and down with excitement in the passenger seat, but she doesn't say a word.

The boys know about the new boat, of course. Last year, over my objections—we already had a three-horsepower Evinrude out-board motor they could put on the wooden rowboat, which I thought was plenty—Bill bought a twelve-horse Elgin from Sears Roebuck and put it on a leaky old wooden Casco Bay boat he'd picked up somewhere, raising the transom and stern gunwales with two-by-fours to accommodate it. Just as I'd warned him, the Elgin was too much motor for that boat; even with Bill's modifica-tions, water sloshed over the transom every time it was shifted out of neutral into forward. After watching the boys nearly swamp the thing one too many times, I put my foot down and told Bill I didn't want them running around the lake another summer in it.

Bill agreed with me about the safety issue, but that was where our consensus ended. My thought was that the boys needed a smaller motor; his idea was to get them a better boat.

They spent the winter poring over boat magazines together and discussing just which model they wanted, although their choices were limited, both by our budget and by the height of Johnny's Bridge, which connects North Pond to Round and South Ponds. The boat they chose needed to be big enough to take the twelve-horse motor, but low enough to fit under the bridge, so that they could take it from camp to Locke's Mills to pick up our mail at the post office, and milk and bread and penny candy at Lee's Variety. It had to be stable and sturdy, and it couldn't cost too much.

In January, Bill took them to the big boat show in New York City, and they settled on a twelve-foot aluminum Duratech Runabout, with an enclosed bow and a steering wheel in front. Bill ordered it in the spring from a boat shop in Westfield, to be delivered to Bethel by train after we had arrived at camp for the summer.

None of the boys has mentioned the boat since their father died, as if it would be wrong to bring it up. But of course I know they haven't forgotten. It's been two weeks since Bill's funeral, and he's about to give his sons one last tangible gift.

Thank you, I say silently to Bill as I park the car, and the boys begin to unload the laundry and groceries, and lug them down the hill to the camp.

"They're good kids, Ruth," Bill says, only to me. "And they're going to have years of fun with that boat; you'll see."

"It was like he was still with us"
Steve, Greg, Andy, Leslie

Greg: 1958 was the year the boat arrived in Bethel on the train in the biggest cardboard box I'd ever seen.

Steve: The boat was a dream of mine all through the winter of 1957-58. Dad took us boys to the boat show in New York City and I had studied boat magazines like crazy. Dad ordered it from a boat shop in Westfield to be delivered to Maine. When it arrived at the Bethel train station by railway express, Albert Buck, who ran the gas station across Railroad Street from the railroad station, loaded it into his pickup truck and brought it down to camp. I think we had purchased the twelve horsepower Elgin outboard from Sears Roebuck the year before and used it on a redesigned Rangeley boat. With the twelve horsepower on the Duratech aluminum boat, we were in contention for fastest on North Pond.

Greg: Steve's memories are good, and not to nitpick, but I believe the boat the Elgin motor was first on (and it was too much motor for it) was actually a Casco Bay boat, with the transom raised somewhat by the addition of two-by-fours. Who remembers when we finally burned that dry rotted old thing years later?

Steve: That was the boat. I guess it was a Casco Bay. In my mind, it had become a Rangeley, because I have this reverence for the classic...1946 Jeep, 1857 farmhouse, old Maine camp, etc. It's a disease. I do remember the winter when Dad created the system to raise the transom and stern gunwales so it wouldn't swamp so easily.

Leslie: Wow. I don't even remember that boat. I guess I was too busy ramming the white wooden boat into Sunny Rock!

Steve: Les, I hereby give you permission to let that bit of guilt go. You must have other things you can put in its place. Anyone who has not banged a boat on a rock or bridge, please raise your hand. (I'm currently sitting on mine!)

Andy: Some vivid memories of the summer of 1958 were linked to the almost magical arrival of our Duratech aluminum boat. I'd forgotten all about the boat, so its arrival was another shock. When a boat Dad bought for us arrived a few weeks after he died, it was like he was still with us and happy to see us play.

July 14, 1958, North Pond, Woodstock, Maine

Ruth

AFTER THREE DAYS OF NEARLY CONSTANT RAIN—three days of Monopoly, Hearts, popcorn, and jigsaw puzzles, of the smells of wet dog and damp socks drying by the stove—I wake up and realize that the patter on the metal roof has ceased sometime in the night. My bedroom on the back of the camp is still in semi-darkness; its only window looks out at the steep banking, and beyond that, on the other side of the road, Moody Mountain rises sharply.

No direct sunlight ever shines into the two tiny downstairs bedrooms, making them perfect for sleeping late, something I've never been able to do, not before Bill's death, and certainly not since.

I can hear the dog snoring lightly on the floor. I began the night with my door closed, because Leslie, who starts out each night in the second bedroom on the other side of the thin wall of tongue-and-groove boards, hopes that if the dog can't sleep in my room, he'll choose to sleep in hers. She's made him a nest on the floor at the foot of the bed, using a low cardboard box and a coarse old green wool Army blanket from the loft that mice have chewed holes in over the winter. She's put a bowl of water beside this makeshift bed and last night at bedtime she lured him into her room with a Milk-Bone and shut the door. He ate the biscuit willingly enough, but then—ungrateful beast—he refused to settle down, scratching at the door until I told her I had to let him out.

"I'll leave your door open, and then maybe he'll come back in after the boys and I go to bed," I told her.

"All right, but shut your door tonight, Mommy. I want him to sleep with me."

"I will."

We got Lucky for the kids four years ago, but he's always considered himself Bill's dog, no matter that I've been firm in my resolve to make it the kids' job to walk and feed and brush him. Before Bill's death, he'd never really warmed up to me, perhaps intuiting that I tolerated, more than welcomed, his presence. Now, though, like Leslie, he can't go more than a few minutes without checking to make sure I'm still here. At meals, he sits at my feet under the table even though I'm the one least likely to slip him a scrap from my plate, and at bedtime he has taken to curling up on the floor just inside the doorway of my bedroom. Last night, encountering my closed door, he whined softly for a few minutes, then I heard him sigh and make his way upstairs to the loft to sleep with the boys.

Back in New Jersey, he sleeps by himself in the kitchen at night and spends too much of his day chained to his doghouse in the backyard. Here at camp, though, he's in heaven, running loose all summer long, wading into the lake on hot days, digging treacherous holes all over the lot that I make the boys fill back in before one of us, on our way to the outhouse in the dark, can step in them and turn an ankle.

If the dog really would sleep with Leslie, maybe she would last all night long in her own room. Now I look at her, sleeping deeply on what I will always think of as Bill's side of the double bed. She woke me sometime in the night—the rain was still falling, but more lightly than when we went to bed—whispering urgently that she had to use the outhouse. The dog came down the narrow stairs from the loft, metal tags jingling, when he heard me get out of bed. I put on my moccasins to walk the thirty yards or so to the little square building and handed Leslie the flashlight with a warning not to lose it down the hole. As I waited for her outside, the darkness enclosed me so completely that when I shut my eyes, then opened them again, I could make out no difference.

While I waited, a loon called, down at Ada's end of the lake, and another answered. Something moved slowly through the woods above the camp, on the other side of the road, snapping twigs as it went. It sounded too small and too cautious to be a bear, and it didn't occur to me to be frightened, only curious, but I was glad I'd made the dog stay inside. I heard him whine and scratch lightly on the door, and I hoped he wouldn't set to barking and wake the boys.

Leslie emerged, the beam of the flashlight cutting through the darkness, and put her hand in mine to stumble sleepily back to the camp. She didn't pause at the doorway of her own room, but went straight past it to mine and climbed into my bed. I didn't argue with her, and she was asleep by the time I'd taken off my moccasins, turned off the flashlight and set it on the dresser, and slid in beside her. I lay awake for a long time, listening to the loons and the light rain on the roof.

When I wake up in the gray half-light and realize the rain has stopped, I know I should get right up and get on with the day. We've barely been able to get outside for the past three days, and there are boats to bail, errands to run, wet towels draped over the railing of the loft that need to be hung on the line if the sun is going to come out at last.

But, like every morning when I awaken, it is as if I am swimming slowly up through deep black water, my thoughts struggling to break the surface. My arms and legs are leaden. A vague nausea still comes upon me in waves as I lie in bed, not as strong as in the first mornings after Bill's death, but still unsettling. I know that once I force myself to get up, and have my coffee and toast, it will disappear, but at the moment it seems far easier to lie perfectly still. I stare at a group of knots on the ceiling as I would fix my gaze on a point on the horizon to avoid seasickness if I were on a ship at sea.

Something—the weight of the blankets, or of the rain-damp air, or of the responsibilities that press down on me during every conscious moment—pins me to the mattress. I know I won't fall back to sleep, but maybe—just once—I'll give in to the heaviness of my limbs and the thickness in my skull, and stay in bed.

What if I never got up, all day? I imagine the slow hours passing, the boys rising, coming down the narrow stairs, bewildered not to find me in the kitchen. I see them making breakfast for themselves and Leslie. I imagine them looking at one another, speaking in low voices, wondering what to do. One of them, probably Steve, maybe Greg, would notice we are almost out of milk, would peer cautiously around the door jamb, whisper that they were taking some money from my wallet to go to the store. I would nod without speaking, and once the sound of the outboard motor had faded, I would relax into the silence, confident that they all had their lifejackets, that Leslie had been securely buckled into hers, that they would remember to pick up the mail and the newspaper and a loaf of bread, if we need one.

Then I would make my mind a blank slate once more, and for a few minutes, or a few hours, it would be as if I had never lost Bill—as if I had never known Bill. I would forget about my children, about the chores and the errands and the wet towels, about everything.

Instead, of course, I swing my heavy legs to the floor, slip out of bed without awakening Leslie, and reach for my jeans and the plaid flannel shirt I wore yesterday. I can tell already that it's going to be warmer today, and I decide against building a fire in the stove, even though the sun, if it comes out, won't shine directly on our side of the lake until nearly noon. I find my old canvas sneakers under the bed and put them on without socks. I ease open the back door and close it quietly behind me, the dog at my heels.

After I use the outhouse, I step across the bridge we've built to connect Sunny Rock to the shore, and look out at the lake. Fog has settled on the surface, and I can't see across to the opposite shore, or even past the swimming float, bobbing on four black-painted metal barrels a few yards from shore. When I turn to look back at the camp, thin wisps of fog drift like cobwebs in front of my eyes. Above the tops of the trees, over the top of Moody Mountain, a brighter spot in the sky tells me the sun is rising, and I wonder if it will burn away the fog, or if the clouds will smother it, and give us yet another rainy day.

I retrace my steps across the bridge, and make my way over rocks and roots to the tiny beach, held in a curve of the shore like a cupped palm. There are high-bush blueberries here, growing wild at the edge of the water. We've done nothing to encourage them except to cut out a few encroaching striped maple shoots, but for two or three weeks each summer they keep us in berries, enough nearly every day to eat on cereal, or to make a batch of muffins or pancakes. Now and then I make a blueberry cake in the dented square baking pan that came to me, along with the recipe, printed on a spattered index card, from Lena's restaurant, when she and Gram finally gave it up, a few years after Bill and I were married.

The berries are slow to ripen this summer, but when they finally do, the rain of the past few days means they'll be plump and juicy. I find two dark blue ones among the tiny green and purple globes and pop them in my mouth, remembering the first berries I tasted from these bushes, on that hot day when we brought the kids to see the camp lot for the first time.

"Close your eyes," Bill said then—can it really be four years ago now?—hiding his hands behind his back. "And open your mouth." I bit down on the sun-warmed berry he placed on my tongue and tasted the burst of juice, at once sweet and tart. If Sunny Rock hadn't already made up our minds about this lot, the blueberries would have done it.

The kids' flat-bottomed rowboat is pulled up on the narrow strip of sand, tied to the hemlock tree above the beach for extra security against the wind and rain of the past few days that threatened to carry it away. A bailer made from a cut-down plastic bleach bottle is floating above the floorboards in the rainwater.

I take off my sneakers and put them on the seat in the bow, roll up the bottoms of my jeans, step over the gunwale into the boat, and begin to bail. The dog watches nervously from the shore, then he jumps in behind me.

In a few minutes I've bailed out most of the water. The wooden oars, conscientiously removed from the oarlocks, are stowed neatly along the sides of the boat, blades resting on the stern seat, the way Bill has taught the kids to place them so they don't come loose and float away.

Without knowing I'm about to do it, I clamber out, untie the rope from the tree, and toss it into the boat. Then, pushing off from the shore, I climb back in. The dog's toenails scrabble briefly on the floorboards as he makes his way to the stern seat, where he often rides as ballast when Leslie practices her rowing. I sit on the center seat, fit the pins of the oars into the locks, and brace my feet against the floorboards.

My first pull sends the boat out past the float, into the fog. My second erases the shoreline, the camp, and Sunny Rock from view. By the time I've taken five or six more strokes, I might as well be out on the ocean, miles from shore, for all I can see of the landscape surrounding the pond. It's as if my eyes have been covered with damp cotton gauze.

Bill and the kids built this wooden rowboat from a kit a few years ago, in the basement of our house in Newington. Under his tutelage, the boys measured and sawed the floorboards and seats, caulked the seams, and painted it, inside and out, with glossy marine paint—white for the body of the boat, and bright red for the oars and trim. The seats and floorboards are held in place by flathead wood screws, hundreds of them. It was Leslie's job—she was only three that winter—to toddle from one to another of the boys, carrying the box of screws, passing them out like a diminutive hostess at a cocktail party with a tray of hors d'oeuvres.

There's an ancient blue three-horse Evinrude outboard motor fastened to the transom that the boys use when they troll for white perch, and I know how to operate it, but this morning I want only the near-silence of the oars as each stroke stirs the surface of the water. I want to feel the tightness in my abdomen and the burn in my arms and shoulders as I take smooth, long pulls, making miniature whirlpools that slip away into the low wake behind the boat.

After a few minutes of strong, rhythmic strokes, I judge myself to be somewhere near the middle of the lake, and I pull harder with the oar in my left hand to turn the boat slightly. Now I am heading in what I think must be the general direction of the row of islands at the southern end of the pond, although I can no longer see the bright spot that marked the eastern sky, and the fog is so thick and disorienting that if it suddenly lifted, I wouldn't be surprised to find myself somewhere else entirely, down at Ada's end instead, or fetching up on the shallow sandbar at the mouth of the brook directly opposite our camp, on the western shore.

Today marks five weeks since Bill's death. In the days since then, it's a rare moment when I'm not performing some prescribed duty, doing something I know is exactly what needs to be done to propel our lives forward. At night, I fall into bed and sleep now, no longer lying awake for hours, because I've exhausted myself with a day of chores and activities and planning. I wake hours before dawn, and, in between revisiting all the details of our life together, of Bill's death, of the future life I imagine, I make detailed plans for the day ahead before I finally force myself to rise.

Determined that the kids' lives will go on as normally as possible, I start each morning with a review of the list of projects Bill had planned to do with them this summer—projects for which none of us have either the heart or the energy now—and, somehow, not wanting to disappoint the others, we each summon the strength to push through them. We get the outhouse painted, finish building the boat dock and attach wooden cleats for tying up the new aluminum boat, cut the encroaching alders back from the beach. We haul dead limbs out of the woods and use the bucksaw to cut them up for firewood and the maul to split the larger pieces; we all work together to stack them against the back wall of the camp, under the overhang of the eaves, handy to the door.

When we can't think of anything else that needs doing, we spend an hour hauling sand from the pile beside the road, bringing it down the steep hill by the wheelbarrow-load to dump into the pond to improve our beach. Just as in previous years, Bill ordered a four-yard load from one-armed Art Kimball in West Paris this spring, calling him from New Jersey just days before he died. The kids and I weren't home at camp the day Art delivered it, but we met him heading back out the road as we were coming in with groceries and spring water. I had to back the car up a tenth of a mile or so, to a place in the road wide enough to let him pass. I rolled down my window and asked if he'd left me a bill.

"Nope, guess I didn't," he said, not meeting my eyes. The stump of his left arm rested on the door of his truck.

"How much do I owe you?"

"Don't worry about it. You don't owe me nothing."

"Don't be ridiculous," I told him. "Tell me what I owe you."

He sighed. "Same as last year—fifty cents a yard for the sand, three-seventy-five a yard for delivery. Seventeen dollars."

I held out a twenty-dollar bill and thanked him.

"I wish you'd just keep that, Mrs. Wight," he pleaded. "I ain't got change anyway."

"I don't want change."

He sighed again, then reached across his body with his good right arm. He took the bill deftly between two fingers, then plucked his wallet from his shirt pocket, flipped it open, and tucked the bill inside. There was a grinding sound and a clunk as he shifted the dump truck into first gear. Still without looking at me, he said, "Me and my wife, we're both awful sorry for your loss." Then he was gone.

I continue to row, taking long, even strokes, pressing lightly against the stern seat with my bare toes as I feel each pull in my arms, legs, and abdomen. The only sounds are the creak of the metal oarlocks, the muffled rushing of the water as it races to fill in the trough behind the stern made by our progress, and the soft sloshing of the remaining rainwater in the bottom of the boat, beneath the floorboards.

I put my back into the rowing, seeing how fast I can make the little wooden boat slip over the water, breathing in time with my strokes, trying to take at least twenty hard pulls before I rest the oars for a moment to catch my breath.

The dog remains upright and attentive in the center of the stern seat, his ears lifted slightly, his eyes on my face. His expression is one of mild concern. Although he is always quick to join the kids on their boating adventures, he is dimly aware that I belong back on the shore, waiting for their return, not out here on the water, and especially not so early in the morning, in such a dense fog.

After several minutes, as I am beginning to wonder where on the lake I am, the white circle of the sun appears again through the fog. It's on my right as I sit facing the stern, so the bow of the boat is pointed south, as I guessed, heading toward the islands. I glance over my shoulder, past the bow, but there is still nothing to see but the thick cotton fog.

For a long time the dog doesn't move, but then, after one set of twenty strokes, he shifts his gaze, looking up and past me with sudden interest. I turn to look over my shoulder, to see what he sees, and the dark shape of Rock Island looms out of the fog above us. Quickly, I raise my oars, then pull hard on the right one to bring the boat parallel with the island and avoid smashing the bow against the rock.

Rock Island is just what its name implies, a vast granite boulder left behind by the glacier whose slow retreat from what is now New England built up its hills and mountains and scraped out its valleys and lakes. Its surface is rounded, smooth, like an enormous turtle shell. Almost the only vegetation is a small white birch tree, clinging to a pocket of soil that has washed or blown here over the course of ten thousand years. That spindly tree, some low, scrubby blueberry bushes, and the few coarse blades of marsh grass that sprout from the damp muck that collects in a tight crack running the length of the island—that's all; the rest is barren rock. The lake's steep drop-off on the south side and the narrow ledge that forms a natural diving platform several feet above the water make it a popular spot for swimming and picnicking on sunny days.

On the side that faces down the lake toward our camp, the boulder that is the island slopes gradually into the water. Freshwater mussels cling to the green-slimed rock surface, and tiny minnows dart here and there beside the rowboat.

The kids have been here a hundred times by boat, sometimes bringing the wicker hamper with a lunch I've packed for them, but, I realize now, I've never set foot on the island myself. I row the boat around to the spot where the blueberry bushes grow and the rock forms a tiny cove, just big enough to nose the bow into. I climb out and loop the painter around the slender birch tree, securing it with two half hitches.

Leaving my sneakers on the bow seat, I clamber barefoot up the steep incline, the granite cool and wet, rough on the soles of my feet. Near the top, two squarish boulders perch, seeming to balance precariously along the sloping backbone of the island, but as solid, in reality, as the enormous rounded one beneath them. From the higher one, a seagull regards me with a malevolent yellow eye, its head cocked to one side, and gives an aggravated squawk before lifting off to disappear into the fog.

One side of the lower boulder is slanted, inviting access to its top, and when I scramble up it, I'm surprised at how easy it is to do. I straighten up and stand there for a few minutes, the dog whining softly from below.

The higher boulder looks to be more of a challenge, its sides nearly perpendicular, with few signs of a toe- or finger-hold that I can see from where I stand now, eye-level with its table-like top. Of course, this is the one I want to conquer, the one on which I want to sit and swing my legs, waiting to see if the fog will burn off and reveal the view from its damp summit.

I half-climb, half-slide down the sloped side of the lower boulder. When I reach the bottom, one foot lands, hard, on a broken mussel-shell, dropped, no doubt, by the irritated seagull. It slices cleanly into the pad of my heel, and I curse the stupid bird as I hobble down to the water's edge, leaving a trail of dark spatters of blood on the rock. The dog follows anxiously, pausing to lick at the drops. I stick my foot in the lake and watch as my blood is carried away in feathery wisps, mixing like red ink with the water.

It's a small cut, really, and the cold water stops most of the bleeding right away. I climb back up the slope to the base of the higher boulder and circle it two or three times, looking for a way up.

I know it can be done, because I've looked out across the water from our camp and seen people up there. The boys have done it—even Leslie has been to the top, although she had to be helped up by two of her brothers.

The side that looked the most promising when I stood looking at it from atop the other boulder proves, after all, to be impossible to scale. I would need a boost, or to be at least a foot taller, to reach the first bit of jutting rock with my toes, and the slight lip of stone near the top that I can just touch by stretching one hand up as far as I can reach is too narrow to get a solid hold on.

Two of the other faces of the boulder are even more forbidding. One is a smooth, unbroken wall of stone; the other offers cracks that at first appear encouraging, but the top overhangs the bottom here, rendering it inaccessible from this side.

On the remaining side, the rock surface below slopes away from the base of the boulder, making it more difficult to reach what appear to be possible handholds. One is an actual knob of stone, good for gripping, but from where I stand, I can just touch the bottom of it with the tips of my fingers. No good.

I try a standing jump, just a little hop at first, self-conscious as if someone were watching, someone besides the dog. I gradually build up to flexing my knees and springing upward as hard as I can, but I'm no basketball player, and this gains me no more than three or four inches, not enough.

At last I try getting a running start, backing off several paces and charging up the slope toward the boulder, leaping as I reach it and stretching both arms over my head, grabbing for the projecting knob. I can feel my hands grasp it firmly, and I think I've got it made, until I try to haul my weight up using just my arms. My feet scrabble uselessly over the rock, unable to find a purchase; I remember that I've never been able to do a pull-up, and realize I'm not going to be able to do one now.

I stand back and study the stone face again, noticing for the first time a tiny irregularity about two and a half feet off the ground. It's a narrow parallel vein of some other kind of rock, lighter-colored, milky quartz, maybe, and it runs in a band all the way across this side of the boulder, protruding maybe half an inch from the granite.

I raise my right foot and can just reach the jutting band with my toes, but without being able to simultaneously pull myself upward with my arms, it does me no good. I'll have to try the running approach again, then hurl myself at the rock, grasping the knob above my head with both hands, while feeling with my bare feet for this slimmest of toeholds.

My first try is a failure, as are the next five, ten, twenty attempts. By now my fingertips are raw from slipping off the rough surface, and the top of my left big toe is bleeding where I've scraped it on the rock searching for the quartz vein. I've slammed the boulder repeatedly with my nose, chin, forehead, elbows, and knees. I am sobbing. My jaw aches from gritting my teeth and the muscles in my arms are burning. The dog has given up his soft whining in favor of yelping in panic each time I smash into the boulder again and slither gracelessly to the base of it.

On what I tell myself will be my final attempt, I leap up and feel my hands close securely around the knob of rock. The toes of first my right foot, then my left, catch on the vein of quartz and somehow I am clinging to the face of the rock, knees spread gracelessly apart, hips pressed painfully against the rough granite. Before I can stop to think or catch my breath, I summon all of my strength and pull myself up with my arms while cautiously lifting one foot, placing the sole against the vertical surface, inching it gradually upward. I follow with the second foot, then, when both feet feel somewhat secure, I will myself to let go with one hand and stretch my arm up toward the top of the rock. My fingers reach the horizontal surface, and I give a mighty pull that threatens to dislocate my shoulder, at the same time straightening my shaking legs, pressing my toes into the rock, imagining my feet covered with suction cups, like the tentacles of an octopus.

I stretch my other arm up and find that I can rest first one elbow, then the other, on the top edge of the boulder, and I know

I've made it. I wriggle and swim the rest of the way up, falling forward onto the flat top and hauling my shaking legs up behind me.

The top of the rock is smooth and wet and littered with bits of mussel shell and slick greenish blobs of seagull excrement. Too weak to stand, I cross my legs and sit near the edge, feeling the dampness and chill seeping through the seat of my jeans, moving up my spine and into my chest. I begin to shiver, and soon my shoulders are shaking with the cold and the effects of the exertion.

The cut on my heel has been bleeding again. Looking down to the rock below me, I see my rusty footprints on its surface, row after row of them, where I ran and leapt against the boulder. They look like trampled rose petals, or brilliant autumn leaves, pressed into the granite. I should get the bailer from the boat and wash them away before I leave.

It feels like hours since I pushed off in the rowboat from the beach at camp, but it can't really have been very long, because the circle of pale light that is the sun is still low in the eastern sky, still obscured by the fog. I expect Leslie and the boys are still sound asleep; I hope so. It will be dark inside the camp for a long time yet. I wrap my arms tightly around myself, trying to get warm.

"You're so stubborn, Ruth," Bill says, admiringly. "Most people would have given up after the first or second try. It's one of the things I love best about you. You don't give up."

His words are like a thick, warm blanket laid over my shoulders. My shivering stops, and I understand why I had to come here, what dragged me to the surface of the dark water of my dreams, pulled me out of bed, drove me to climb to the top of this rock, at the top of this island.

"I'll never give up," I promise.

For the rest of my life, I'll be speaking to him, and listening for what he has to tell me. This, now, is what prayer is to me.

My Mother's Journal
May 2008

Amy

I'M SITTING ON THE DECK AT CAMP. A breeze from the northwest is keeping most of the blackflies away, and bringing perfect mid-spring weather—dry air, cloudless skies, and just enough of a residual nip in the air to make me glad I wore a sweatshirt.

I came here this morning to start getting the camp ready for summer—to make up a few of the beds, to open the windows and let in some fresh air, and, especially, to rid the place of a winter's accumulation of mouse residue: nesting material, forgotten stores of seeds, and the ubiquitous droppings.

I brought the good vacuum cleaner from home, some sponges and rags and cleaning products, and a bucket I intended to use to haul water from the lake to heat on the stove. I planned to vacuum everything first—floors, furniture, countertops, and shelves—then clean the kitchen cupboards with hot water, giving everything a good final going-over with a bleach solution.

It's a routine I follow every year, because in my head I hear my mother telling me that this is what I need to do. Then I can say I've done it, and tell myself everything has been properly cleaned, although I know the minute the clean dishes are replaced in the disinfected cupboards and my back is turned, the mice are back at it, scampering up the wall, squeezing into the cupboards, and running across the stacks of plates.

The only solution to the mouse problem is a good cat or two, and we will bring ours with us when we move to camp for the summer. They'll keep the mice at bay, at least until we leave in the fall.

As soon as I arrived, though, I realized that it was too perfect a day to work indoors.

"It doesn't matter what you do," my mother's voice told me, "as long as you keep going. It all needs to get done."

So, instead, I spent an hour cleaning the deck, bringing out the porch furniture, sweeping cobwebs off the shingle siding, and washing the outsides of the windows. Then I sat down in the sun with the lunch I brought, and here I am now, sitting on the deck, eating yogurt with strawberries, watermelon, and the occasional errant blackfly.

It's a privilege to be here all alone, without even the dog, who went to work in the woods with Tony this morning. One other camp on the road is occupied, but it's far enough away from ours that I might as well be the only one on this side of the lake today.

I've been reading my mother's journal on these days when I can steal a little time alone here. We found it four years ago, after she died, on a bookshelf here at camp. It begins in June of 1982, as she prepared for her move from Connecticut to Bethel upon her retirement as a school librarian, and continues for about three and a half years.

Although my grandfather kept a diary throughout his adult life—assiduously noting, in brief entries devoid of emotion, events as mundane as "Worked around home; mowed lawn" and as shattering as "Laura [my grandmother] died today"—as far as any of us know, this was the only time in her life when his daughter kept any sort of journal. We don't know how she happened to stop writing, except that her so-called retirement had, after a few years, gotten so busy that she probably just didn't have the time.

In perfect keeping with my mother's frugal nature, this journal consists of an assortment of looseleaf notebook pages—some wide-ruled, some college-ruled, no doubt left over from other endeavors—in a white plastic three-ring binder with advertising on the cover: "Swagelok—Tube Fittings and Quick-Connects" and "Cajon—Vacuum Couplings, Precision Pipe and Weld Fittings."

I suppose that all of us who keep a journal, even if we never intend for it to see the light of day, have some sort of audience in mind. We may write for our children, in the hope that our words will build a bridge for them to their past, or for future admirers of our work who may someday thrill to our most personal words after we've become famous. We may write to inform another, less enlightened side of ourselves, to channel thoughts we didn't know we had until we picked up a pen and sat alone with them.

When my mother wrote in her journal, she was speaking to my father, who, when she began writing, had been dead for nearly a quarter of a century. Her first entry, on June 22, 1982, begins, "Your 70th birthday, Bill, and a very good day to close out my Milford life and get ready to carry out our dream of retirement on a hill in Bethel!"

Married for only sixteen years, and a widow until her own death forty-six years later, still my mother lived out her life as my father's wife. She had with him, we now know, a constant exchange of thoughts, an inner dialogue that spanned the decades. Just as she had always done during his brief life, she shared with him her aspirations, ambitions, and ideas, and she drew courage and solace from their conversations.

Now she tells me that it's time to get back to work.

"Don't let the afternoon get away from you."

"Thanks, Mom," I say out loud.

Summer 1958, North Pond, Woodstock, Maine

Ruth

WE KEEP TO OURSELVES, FOR THE MOST PART, and soon there is a rhythm to our days at the lake, days that are, in fact, not so very different from the ones the kids and I have spent here over the past three summers, during the week, when Bill was working in New Jersey. I rise and put the coffee on. After a while, the boys straggle down the narrow stairs from the loft; Leslie emerges, tousled and rubbing her eyes. We eat breakfast at the broad oak table in front of the windows that face the lake.

Some mornings I swim before the kids are awake, plunging into the cool water and kicking my way out past the float while the dog, a poor excuse for a spaniel, wades in after me but stops when the water reaches his belly and regards me anxiously. If there is no wind and the surface of the water is as smooth as glass, I swim far out into the pond with a determined breast stroke, then turn over onto my back and float, arms outstretched.

We devote our mornings to projects and continue to make headway on Bill's list, still tacked to the wall beside the old-fashioned crank phone, where he put it last September as we packed up to leave. Looking at it, written in his small, tidy handwriting, leads me to think of the silly notes he used to leave around the house for me in the early years of our marriage, and to wish I had saved them.

"Here's looking at you, kid," I found taped to the bathroom mirror.

Clipped to the clothesline when I went out to hang the wash on a weekday morning: "Wish I were hanging around with you today."

"This is just to say," he wrote on a scrap of paper I found on the breakfast table once when he'd left the house early for a morning business meeting and let me sleep, "I have eaten the last slice of custard pie that was in the icebox, and which you were probably saving for lunch. Forgive me. It was delicious, so sweet and so cold."

Later, if it's a nice day, the kids take the boat to Locke's Mills for the mail and groceries, and while they are gone I mix up a batch of cookies or brownies and put them in the oven, or a blueberry cake. When they return I make a stack of bologna or egg salad or peanut butter and jelly sandwiches for lunch, slice them on the diagonal, and nibble at a small triangle of one while they devour the rest.

If it's raining, there are cards and puzzles and board games to fill the day, and a bookcase full of cast-off children's classics to reread—*Little Women*, *The Five Little Peppers*, *Tom Sawyer*. I might take the car to the store and post office if the weather keeps the kids from going by boat, or, if we have enough milk and bread, I might decide I can live without the daily paper and any mail that might be waiting for us, addressed simply to "General Delivery, Locke's Mills, Maine."

Rain or shine, I spend most of the afternoon hours reading—the newspaper, a stack of magazines I've brought with me from Westfield, or a novel. On nice days, the kids swim and run around the lake in their new boat. I go in for a swim, too, in the late afternoon, and then it's time to start supper. Evenings, it's Scrabble or Monopoly, with the Red Sox on the crackly brown Bakelite radio. The station closest to us, WRUM in Rumford, goes off the air at night, but late in the evenings we can sometimes pick up the games from as far away as Boston, or even on WTIC in Hartford.

The days pass.

In mid-August, Don and Leota and the kids come for a visit. Don has called me every Sunday evening since Bill died—almost the only times we hear our ring, one long and four short, on the party line—and although I've tried to reassure him, I think they have both been imagining the worst. They seem relieved to see how well we're doing, that the camp is not falling down around us, that there are meals on the table and cookies in the cookie jar.

Leslie finds Barbara to be an ideal playmate—old enough to play games with her, but young enough to let her decide which ones. In fact, all of the kids have a wonderful time with their cousins, and it does us adults good to hear them laugh together. My father has asked me to send Leslie for a visit when Don and Leota leave on Sunday to spend the rest of their vacation in Bangor, and, much to my surprise, she agrees to go.

A few days before Don and Leota's arrival, she had sliced open the bottom of her heel, stepping on a mussel shell under the water. The edges of the cut were clean, and it bled enough so that after I had dabbed it with Mercurochrome and bandaged it, I didn't worry much about it; I was confident it would heal quickly without becoming infected. But after breakfast on Sunday, as Leota is gathering their things to leave, I notice that Leslie is limping slightly, and when I sit her down and pull off her sneaker and sock to change the bandage, I'm surprised to find that the heel is red, and hot to my touch.

"Ouch, Mommy, don't!" she says when I press on the puffy flesh beside the cut, which is still oozing slightly, not yet closed up. I wonder if I should have taken her for stitches when it happened a week ago, but it was a relatively small cut, not terribly deep, and no more severe than a dozen others I'd treated and forgotten this summer.

"It's okay," she insists. "It doesn't hurt that much. I think it's getting better." So I apply more Mercurochrome, cover the cut with a fresh bandage, and help her pack her small duffel bag for the trip.

"The boys and I will come to Grampa's for a couple of days next week, and bring you back to camp then," I tell her, and she nods and waves bravely from the back of Don's station wagon, where, amid the suitcases, she and Barbara are putting their baby dolls to bed in an empty cardboard box.

Late Wednesday morning, after the boys return in the boat from Locke's Mills, where they've picked up the mail and a few groceries to tide us over until our next trip to Bethel, I suggest a picnic lunch on Buck's Ledge. I haven't been up yet this summer, although the kids, even Leslie, have made several climbs to the top of the sheer cliff overlooking the pond.

After a couple of overcast days, today there is barely a cloud in the sky. I pack sandwiches, apples, and some of the snickerdoodle cookies I made while the boys were gone to town into a canvas knapsack and fill two Army surplus canteens with cool water from the spring.

As we start up the steep trail behind the camp, I am thinking about the last time I hiked up Moody Mountain to the ledges. It was after supper at sunset, on the evening before we left Maine at the beginning of last September, with Bill and all the kids. At my insistence, we had each carried a flashlight, but even after we sat together on the cooling granite and watched until the last of the orange glow had left the western sky, there was enough light left for the short descent, barely half a mile.

Today the sun is directly overhead when we reach the open ledges, and I can smell the sweet late-summer scents of drying ferns and overripe blueberries. When I sit down to open the knapsack, I feel the heat from the smooth gray rock through the worn seat of my jeans. Sweat from the exertion of the climb trickles down my temples, and I tip my head back to let the sun's rays and the slight breeze dry my face.

While Leslie is gone, I sleep later, stretched out across the bed. The early-morning nausea I've felt most mornings since Bill died has eased somewhat, and my appetite has begun to return. In fact, on some days I'm surprised by how hungry I am.

I've been waiting all summer for my menstrual cycle to resume, but I wasn't surprised by its sudden cessation. For most of my adult life, I've been able to predict my periods by consulting the calendar for the date of the full moon. Every month, as the waxing moon gained fullness, so did my body, preparing to shed its ripening, superfluous egg.

In July, as the kids and I sat on Sunny Rock after dark to watch the stars come out, and waited as the yellow full moon rose behind us until we could see its reflection in the lake, I felt none of the usual signs that my period was near. It was to be expected, I thought, that I should skip a month or two. For weeks, I had lived on black coffee and dry toast, and between the shock of Bill's death and my inability to eat, I assumed my cycle had just been interrupted.

Now, however, I'm not so sure.

Buck's Ledge

Amy

I AM LYING ON BUCK'S LEDGE, feeling the curve of the earth in the sun-warmed rock beneath my back. Here and there, in the crevices of the granite, enough soil has accumulated for patches of soft moss to grow, and I am resting my head on one of these, while my heels are braced lightly against a small outcropping of rock. If I turn my head I can see, inches from my eyes, three different varieties of moss. I search lazily through my mental catalog to see if I can name them all, but I can remember only that the tallest one, with its delicate stalks tipped with brilliant red, is called something like British soldier moss.

It is summer, and I have climbed Moody Mountain to see if the blackberries are ripe, and if perhaps I might see a deer or even a moose in the cool, swampy spot behind the ledges that never quite goes dry, even in August. But there are no deer trampling the dark mud today, and no moose, and if there were any ripe blackberries, a bear has gotten here before me and cleaned them out, leaving behind black scat that is pebbled with seeds. I don't mind, because really, I came here to do just what I am doing, to lie on the bare rock that is like a portion of the earth's skeleton exposed, closing my eyes so that I can feel the motion of the planet turning, and opening them to look at the dome of the sky stretching over me and down to the horizon.

As a child, I believed that our world—a sphere, as I understood it to be from the globe my older brothers kept in their bedroom and sometimes referred to for their geography homework—existed inside of another, bigger sphere. I imagined that this larger globe was made of something like opaque blue glass, for it was clear to me that when I looked up at the sky, I was seeing the surface of something blue and solid. All of our weather, I reasoned, took place inside this blue sphere. The sun shone or was obscured by clouds; rain or snow or sleet fell from weather systems that moved about just beneath the impermeable layer that imprisoned our world, or shielded it from what lay beyond.

What lay beyond, I thought most of the time, was probably Heaven, the Heaven I heard about at Sunday school, where the boss of Heaven, God, lived and ate and slept and walked around like a regular person, where I would go after I died—if I was at least pretty well-behaved—and where I would get a chance to meet my father, who was an angel, for the first time and see if, as people told me, I really looked like him.

At times I wasn't so sure about Heaven—who, after all, could prove it was up there? At those times I imagined what was beyond the blue glass to be nothingness, dark and scary and perhaps filled with a whooshing, screeching cacophony of noise.

By the time I was old enough to climb up to Buck's Ledge alone, I was old enough to know something about the solar system and the galaxy and the effect of light coming through the earth's atmosphere, making the sky appear blue. I had a rudimentary understanding—although quite possibly a clearer understanding than I have today—about the difference between the body and the soul, the physical and the spiritual, and that Heaven wasn't a place just above the blue glass where people continued their lives as if they had never been interrupted by death.

Still, whenever I climb the mountain and lie against the curving ledge, and look at the sky—which is not only above me, but all around me, on all sides of the mountaintop—it is easier to believe in a solid, protective layer that safeguards me from the unknown, than to force my mind to bend itself around the notion of uncharted space and infinite distance.

August 1958

From the Diaries of Leon G. White, Bangor, Maine

Sunday, August 17: Beautiful day. Went to Jonesport for blueberries. Got 12 quarts. Leslie came.

Wednesday, August 20: Sandy Point Beach for picnic. Donald and children and Leslie. Beautiful day.

Saturday, August 23: Beautiful day. Worked around home and Leslie and I took a walk.

Sunday, August 24: Cloudy in a.m. but turned out to be a nice day. S, M and Leslie went to Jonesport.

Tuesday, August 26: Gilbert put muffler on car. I mowed lawn, etc. Took Leslie to Dr. for foot infection.

Wednesday, August 27: Ruth and boys arrived in p.m. Nice day.

Thursday, August 28: To Greenville, Pittston Farm, Rip Dam, Millinocket – home via Lincoln. Steve, Greg, and Andy with me.

Friday, August 29: Cloudy. Hurricane "Daisy" expected to arrive today. Ruth went to Bethel in p.m.

August 28, 1958, Bangor, Maine

Ruth

I AM MOMENTARILY DISORIENTED WHEN I wake on Thursday morning to the sun streaming through white lace curtains and the sound of a car passing by on the street below, instead of the quiet darkness of my bedroom at camp. The white sheets and hobnail bedspread under which I am lying feel scratchy against my skin; when I turn over in bed, they give off a faint odor of bleach.

Then I recall the three-hour drive to Bangor yesterday afternoon, arriving in time for the supper my father's housekeeper, Kathleen, had prepared—fish chowder and blueberry muffins, bread-and-butter pickles in my mother's cut-glass bowl, a plate of soft, spicy molasses cookies for dessert.

After supper, Leslie and the boys went next door to visit Nanny Hayes, whose house is always as busy and noisy with her grandchildren and their friends as it was with her own children and theirs when I was growing up here on Boutelle Road. Kathleen busied herself with the dishes, refusing my help, and my father steered me to the green wooden rockers on the front porch.

We sat in silence, listening to the summer evening sounds of the neighborhood. After a few minutes, my father cleared his throat.

"You'll need to be thinking about what to do," he said, as if the thought hadn't occurred to me.

"I know. I have been. I haven't decided anything yet."

"I think it would be best if you moved home."

My father said this abruptly, as if he were talking to the daughter I once was, not the nearly middle-aged woman who had left this house more than twenty years ago.

"I can't do that, Dad. Not with four kids in tow." Dismayed at the very suggestion, I answered too brusquely, then tried to soften my response. "But thank you. I know you want to help, and I do appreciate that."

In the other twin bed, Leslie stirs, opens her eyes, and stretches.

"What are we going to do today, Mommy?" she asks.

"Well, we'll get up and have breakfast and then we can decide."

"Can we go to see Laura and Elaine?"

"Of course we can."

My brother Gib's girls are several years younger than Leslie, Laura just four this year and Elaine still a baby, both of them too young, really, for her to play with. But when we visit, she loves to mother them, reading to Laura and brushing her long dark hair, pushing Elaine around Gib and Joyce's neighborhood in her stroller.

Now she sits on the edge of the high twin bed in her summer pajamas, swinging her bare feet. The sight of a fresh white bandage on her left heel fills me with guilt. Instead of getting better, as I'd hoped, the infected cut had only worsened after she got here, until finally, just yesterday, my father had taken her to see a doctor for it, something I probably should have done myself two weeks ago.

"You know what, Mommy?" Leslie says thoughtfully. "I really wish I could have a little sister."

I don't know what to say to this, so for a minute I say nothing. Then I smile and say, "You love taking care of babies, don't you?" adding briskly, "Now let's get dressed and go have breakfast."

My father and the boys are already up and gone. In the kitchen, Kathleen is washing the dishes from the breakfast they ate shortly after sunrise. She packed them a lunch; they'll be gone all day. Dad has taken them on a tour of some of the sites he visited regularly during his nearly forty years as supervisor of woods clerks for Great Northern Paper Company. He retired when he turned sixty-five in March, but whenever he gets into his car, he says, it still points itself north.

Today they'll head first for Greenville, then to Pittston Farm, Great Northern's remote outpost twenty miles north of Rockwood, where my father often stayed when he was making his rounds of the company's mills and logging camps. A series of rough dirt roads will take them along the shores of Seboomook Lake and the West Branch of the Penobscot River, on to Ripogenus Dam and then to Millinocket, where Dad will point out the paper mill, once the largest in the world, and the elegant Great Northern Hotel, built at the turn of the century to house upper management and other important guests. They'll cover at least three hundred miles and get home after dark, the car caked with mud and dust.

I remember taking the same trip with him a few times as a child when he was making a day trip, and once when we stayed overnight at Pittston Farm. More often, though, it was my brothers, even though they were younger, who got the privilege of accompanying him.

That was how it was when I was growing up. There were the things boys did, and the things girls did. Once every two or three years, my father would buy four tickets to see the Red Sox play at Fenway Park, and he and my brothers would make the trip to Boston by train. He never asked me if I wanted to go with them, and I never mentioned it, either, even though I was as much a baseball fan as the boys, and rarely missed an evening around the radio with them during the season.

Girls learned to cook and sew, and helped to take care of younger siblings. There were occasional outings, too, of course—the most memorable, for me, were annual Christmas shopping trips with my mother to Freese's department store, downtown. We took the trolley from the end of our street and, after browsing floor after floor of toys, clothing, housewares, and furniture, we made our small purchases—a tie for my father, new shirts and a toy or game for Shume and Don. Then we would climb up onto the high stools at the lunch counter and order a grilled cheese sandwich or a chicken salad plate.

In 1929, the year I was nine, Gib was born on the sixth of December. When they came home from the hospital, my mother was quiet and pale and needed to rest a lot. We didn't make our usual trip to Freese's that year.

"We'll go later on, maybe to buy you an Easter dress," she told me, but even by April, she was still too weak to leave the house often. I didn't mention it to her again, and of course I never said anything to my father the next year, when our first Christmas without her approached, or any year after that.

One December Saturday when I was in high school, I took myself downtown on the trolley and walked up Main Street to Freese's. I had a little spending money and was thinking that I'd look for gifts for my father and brothers, then treat myself to a sandwich at the lunch counter. But as soon as I stepped inside, I knew it was a mistake. The store was crowded with shoppers, Christmas carols were playing over the loudspeakers, and everywhere I looked, mothers held small daughters by the hand as they gazed at the holiday displays. I turned swiftly and walked back out through the wide front doors, tears stinging my eyes.

Grampa

Steve, Greg, Andy, Leslie

Greg: In August, the summer after Dad died, Leslie spent a week in Bangor with Grampa, then we went with Mom to pick her up. Leslie had a persistent infection that summer. I remember Mom lancing her calf at the lake and draining pus into the water.

Leslie: I had a persistent staph infection for a long time. Every cut became infected. The foot cut might have started the whole mess. I had cut the bottom of my foot on a mussel shell before going to Grampa's. He took me to the doctor in Bangor. Infections continued after we returned to Westfield. Chicken pox was a nightmare! One in my knee got so bad that Steve and Greg had to make a four-hand seat and carry me downstairs because it was too swollen to support any weight. Finally, after we moved to Milford, a doctor gave me a strong prescription that wiped it out.

Andy: Leslie, I forgot your infections of that summer. Do you suppose that was your body's way of wrestling with Dad's death on a cellular level? Sounds like a Stephen King plot line!

Greg: Grampa took us boys on a tour of some of the Great Northern Paper Company sites in the north woods. I remember that he had a .22 rifle, spotted a woodchuck, and stopped so Steve could shoot it. It ran into a hole where you could see it. Steve shot it in the hole, then felt awful.

Steve: I did get the job of shooting a woodchuck when we were visiting Grampa's old haunts, and yes, I didn't like it. I shot him once and he managed to get himself into a pothole and Grampa insisted that I shoot him again which I did, from two feet away. I never really got over that; I have shot some here, but not at such a close range!

Andy: I remember so little of that summer that I suspect I was pretty much in grief-shock. Grampa did take us to the GNP Company north woods, but I don't recall much; how could I have missed the woodchuck shooting?! I do remember going there again with just Greg and Grampa, maybe the next summer, and he stopped at a shack where an old friend lived to drop off a couple of bottles in a brown bag while we waited in the car. He probably shared a sip with his friend.

It seems that Grampa really stepped up to help Mom after Dad died, and did so in ways that provided what she must have desperately needed—respite from taking care of all of us 24-7. He did what he could uniquely provide—long day trips to visit his former stomping grounds in the north woods on logging roads, log drives on the Penobscot, boom-jumping boats, etc. I also remember visiting in Bangor several summers at the time when the Maine State Fair was on. Greg and I had freedom (and some pocket cash) to wander the fairgrounds—pretty loose for a Grampa who tended to keep close watch on us.

September 2–3, 1958, North Pond, Woodstock, Maine

Ruth

LABOR DAY IS EARLY, SEPTEMBER FIRST, and school won't start until the following Monday, so I decide to wait until Wednesday to leave for Westfield. My father drives over from Bangor on Tuesday morning to help us close up the camp, arriving, after a three-hour drive, just as we are finishing breakfast.

I tell the kids to leave the dishes for me, and take the boat to Locke's Mills to get the mail and the paper. I can tell that my father disapproves. There is plenty they could be doing to help get the camp ready for winter. The float and the dock need to be taken out of the water, the boats stowed away, the waterline pulled from the lake and drained.

But I know they need this last hour of freedom, this last trip of the year in the new boat before they pull the gas line from the motor, unfasten it from the stern and carry it up from the shore. There is a strong breeze this morning, making small whitecaps on the water, and I hope the boys will take an extra lap around the pond before they return. I hope they will open the motor up wide and feel the bow rise and fall as it pounds over the waves. I hope Leslie will feel the wind in her hair. I hope she will squeal with delight one more time.

When the kids return, the six of us work together through the afternoon, and we finish everything that needs to be done by dinnertime. Kathleen has sent over a chicken pie for our last supper at camp, and I use up what's left of a tired head of lettuce to make a salad, adding a tomato and a cucumber I got from Bill's cousin Raymond, at his farm in East Bethel, where we've gone often over the past month to buy corn.

I prefer to stop early in the day, when Raymond is in the fields and Beatrice is busy in the farmhouse, dropping my money into a coffee can on the table beside the driveway where they set up a makeshift farm stand during corn season. This is not because I don't want to see them, but because if we stop in the late afternoon, when either of them is out at the stand, they try not to let me pay. But yesterday morning, when Leslie and I stopped by after we'd been in Bethel to have Raymond's brother, Albert, change the oil in the car before our trip, the driveway was full of Labor Day customers, and both Raymond and Beatrice were sitting behind the table in the shade of the big oak tree.

I let Leslie pick out a dozen ears of corn, and Beatrice reminded her that she should take an extra ear, to make a baker's dozen, she said. She was busy making change for the other customers from the pocket of her apron, and when I handed her my three quarters and quickly stepped away, she sighed and tucked them into the pocket without an argument. But as we started for the car, Raymond stopped us, handing me a paper bag into which he'd dropped a few small pickling cukes and three beautiful ripe tomatoes.

"Headed south soon?" he asked, and I nodded.

"On Wednesday," I said. "Bucky's just changed the car's oil for me."

"Ayuh," he said. "Well, you all have a good winter."

"Yes, and you, too."

Remembering how he rode all the way to New Jersey in June with his brother and two of Bill's old friends to attend the funeral, maybe the furthest he'd ever been from the farm, I suddenly wanted to say more, or even to give him a hug, but of course I didn't. Instead, I just said, "Thank you, Raymond," and patted his arm awkwardly.

Back at camp, we sat on the porch and ate cucumber and tomato sandwiches on squishy white storebought bread from Lee's Variety, and no lunch ever tasted better.

When I awaken on Wednesday morning, the first thing I notice is that I'm cold. The floor feels icy under my bare feet, and I hurry to dress and put on socks and shoes. The thermometer outside the kitchen window reads forty-three degrees, the coldest morning we've had here this summer.

If we weren't heading home today, I'd build a fire in the wood stove and make oatmeal and hot cocoa for the kids. But I've been conscious of trying to use up as much of the remaining food as I can over the past week or so, and this morning we'll make do with Shredded Wheat biscuits soaked in milk and topped with a few ripe blackberries I've picked along the camp road. With luck, we'll be on the road in a couple of hours.

My father is already up, dressed in a plaid wool hunting shirt like the ones Bill wore on chilly mornings at camp. Through the front windows, I can see him standing outside on the porch, looking out at the lake, watching as fog rises from the water.

When I join him there, I say, "The fog on a cool morning like this makes me realize that summer is rising up and leaving the pond."

He nods. "Time for you to be getting back home." Then, "What will you do, Ruth?"

What will I do?

"I don't know," I say honestly. "The kids will go back to school. Winnie's going to live with us for a while. That will help a little with the bills, and she'll be there in the evenings if I need to go out."

Shortly before Bill died, I'd been elected to serve as secretary to the PTA board at the elementary school, and I'm also a member of our church's Christian education committee. Between them, there will be at least three meetings a month. Probably no one would think less of me if I told them I needed to step down from both, but I haven't considered it. They're important responsibilities and, besides, the thought of spending a little time with other adults now and then is not unwelcome.

"I'll come to you for Christmas," my father says suddenly.

"We'd all like that, Dad," I say. He's standing beside me, close enough for me to feel the warm pressure of his shoulder against mine.

"Well, we'd best get you ready to go," he says.

End of summer, 1958

Andy, Leslie

Leslie: The thing I remember about 1958 is that we whipped off to Maine and kind of hibernated at camp all summer. I remember going shopping for back-to-school stuff late that summer, and walking past a huge display of round plastic hoops. When I asked Mom what they were, she said they were probably something for the garden. Who would have guessed than an eight-year-old girl could have been so sheltered that she'd missed the start of the Great Hula Hoop Craze?

Andy: I was glad to read in Grampa's diary that he came to help Mom close the camp. That had to have been a horribly wrenching time for her: leaving Maine, going back to the New Jersey house, suspecting she was pregnant? Like glass? I wonder if she felt at that point that she was walking on broken glass?

September 24, 1958, Westfield, New Jersey

Ruth

THE WAITING ROOM IS STIFLING, crowded—women with babies, mostly, but a few with older children, one middle-aged man, and a heavily pregnant woman perhaps fifteen years younger than me. Dr. Hatch is a family practitioner—he has treated everyone from the squalling infant twins down our street to Grammy, while she lived with us. Not for the ongoing problems with her hip, which had sustained such a complicated break that it required an expensive specialist, but for her occasional colds and the tummy troubles she said came with her adjustment from good Maine well water to our flat, chlorinated, de-mineralized New Jersey tap water.

When my name is called, I follow the doctor's efficient ramrod of a nurse through a swinging door and down a stark white hallway. She stops outside the door of the rest room.

"Do you think you can provide a urine sample this morning?" she asks, and I nod, wondering what she would do if I said no. She ushers me into the tiny room and hands me a glass beaker on the side of which she has written my name in grease pencil. She points to a shelf beside the toilet. "Leave it there when you're done. Don't bring it out with you," she says firmly before she goes out and shuts the door behind her.

The emphasis on this last directive makes me imagine a long line of patients before me who, ignoring her instructions, wandered out into the hallway carrying their full beakers with them, perhaps sloshing their steaming yellow contents onto the carpeted floor.

Lately, the capacity of my bladder seems to have shrunk dramatically, sending me to the bathroom every hour or two, and thanks to my morning coffee, I have no problem producing the required sample, which I set securely on the shelf.

In the hall, the nurse is waiting for me. We pause outside the exam room, at the scale, and, automatically, I slip off my shoes before stepping on. Normally, when I know I'm going to be weighed at the doctor's office, I carefully select an outfit from among the lightest-weight clothes I can find in my closet.

It's silly vanity, not wanting the doctor to think I've put on a pound or two. In truth, except for during my four pregnancies, when I gained the prescribed eighteen pounds—never more than twenty—my weight hasn't changed since high school. Still, I've always felt a little humiliated by the scale—which reads one hundred and sixty pounds, year after year—because, even though I'm tall, it seems like a big number. My father has always told me I am "built like a farm girl," like his own mother, who cut hay with a scythe and raked wild blueberries beside her husband at their saltwater farm in Jonesport.

Now I realize that on this cool late-September morning I've worn a heavier cardigan than I would have chosen if I had given it any thought at all. Removing it would require undoing several buttons, and the nurse is nearly tapping her foot with impatience, so I leave it on.

But even with the heavy sweater, when she calls out my weight, loudly enough for everyone in the waiting room to hear, it's only a hundred and forty-six, a full fourteen pounds less than the last time I was here, when I sprained my ankle back in April, a lifetime ago. All summer, wearing my old camp clothes—loose shirts and baggy jeans—I've paid little attention to how they fit, and although I've noticed the clothes I returned to in New Jersey seemed looser than I remembered, I've been too distracted to think much about it.

Startled by the number, I'm about to mentally congratulate myself, when I remember the reason my weight is down—hardly anything to eat on most days for the first two months after Bill died—and the reason I'm here today. If what I've begun to suspect turns out to be true, this weight loss is cause more for alarm than celebration.

But how can I be right? More likely, my symptoms—an ever-present queasiness, more pronounced in the early mornings, my sleeplessness and frequent exhaustion, and the sudden cessation of my periods after I stopped eating almost entirely for a while back in June—are the result of a poor diet and an excess of black coffee, which, on many of the most difficult days, is still the only thing that sustains me.

As soon as the heavy white door of Exam Room Number Two clicks shut behind me, I strip quickly and get into the cotton gown as fast as I can, so I'll be covered by the time Dr. Hatch pushes his way into the room, already in mid-sentence, knocking as an afterthought.

It has taken a couple of weeks for me to get this appointment. When I called to make it, I didn't say why I needed to come in, only that I hadn't been feeling quite myself for some time and thought a thorough physical was probably in order. I haven't seen Dr. Hatch since the night Bill died, when his eyes were kind and sad as he patted my arm and took charge of the phone calls I couldn't have made myself.

Today his shiny round face is beaming, but despite the crinkling around his eyes, I can see concern behind the smile. As I perch at the edge of the exam table, pulling the skimpy gown tightly around me, he seats himself on a metal stool and begins to ask questions: "How have you been feeling?" and "Are you sleeping well?" and "How are your nerves holding up?"

"Terrible," I want to say, and "I haven't slept more than four hours a night in over three months," and "How do you suppose my nerves are holding up, with a house and four children and a dog to worry about?"

Instead, I tell him that I'm doing fine, really, I'm just a little concerned that something could be the matter, physically, since I haven't had my menses since—oh, sometime in the middle of May, I think it was. I've had a little trouble sleeping, nothing I'm very concerned about. Also, I tell him, until quite recently I haven't felt like eating much; I've lost some weight, which isn't a big problem in itself, of course, since I had some I could stand to lose, but...

The doctor nods to everything I say. "Let's just see how things look, shall we?" We'll rule out a few things, he says, and then perhaps we should talk about a prescription—a sleeping pill, perhaps, or something for anxiety; have I heard of Miltown?

Of course I've heard of Miltown. There was an article in *Time* magazine a few years ago called "Pills for the Mind," about research into how pills and injections can be used to treat all kinds of psychological conditions, just the way penicillin is used to treat physical illnesses and infections. But I have no intention of leaving Dr. Hatch's office with a prescription for it, or for a sleeping pill, or for anything else.

If there's one thing I know, it's that life can be a struggle. It can knock you flat without any warning. Without any warning at all. You have to accept it, even expect it: there are going to be times in your life when a nervous breakdown seems very tempting.

But when it comes to dealing with life's inevitable tragedies and hardships, the thing to do—the only thing to do—is to keep right on getting up in the morning, putting one foot in front of the other, and doing what needs to be done.

It's true that I've felt exhausted, that I haven't been sleeping well since Bill died, but I know that's something that will pass eventually. I've gradually gone from sleeping an hour or two a night to, now, as much as three or four, and the nights when I sleep the most soundly are the ones following the days when I keep myself the busiest. So I've already figured out that the cure for that complaint is simply time and hard work.

As for my other complaint—the persistent nausea—it has continued to improve in these last two weeks, since I made this appointment. It was at its peak in the weeks immediately following Bill's death, and has gradually lessened since then. In fact, I'm back to eating breakfast—toast, orange juice, and black coffee—nearly every morning, with only an occasional lurching in my stomach, and no vomiting at all.

While I've been thinking all of this, making my mind stay busy to keep it off my embarrassment about the physical exam, Dr. Hatch has been listening with his stethoscope to my back and chest, asking me to breathe deeply, shining a light in my ears and nose, using a tongue depressor to examine my throat.

At some point, the nurse has slipped back into the room. She helps me slide my bottom down to the end of the examination table and pats my shoulder in a way meant to seem sympathetic or reassuring, as if to convey that, as humiliating and bizarre and invasive as a pelvic exam may seem to me, Dr. Hatch has performed so many of them that it's no more personal to him than tapping my knees to test my reflexes. Then she expertly maneuvers my feet into the stirrups at the foot of the table, so that I am splayed like the chicken I cut up last night for dinner.

As I lie there, I suddenly know without a shred of doubt, even before Dr. Hatch peers into his speculum, what he is going to tell me. After all, it's not as if I haven't felt all of these things before—the nausea, the tiredness, the inability to sleep through the night. In fact, I've been through this four times before. Never mind that it's been more than nine years since I felt this way. Never mind that any—no, all—of these symptoms could just as easily have resulted from the upheaval of my sudden widowhood.

I know.

But this time it seems impossible to believe. It's so devastating, and yet at the same time so exhilarating, that I can't quite get myself to accept the truth, even when Dr. Hatch, prodding my insides with his chubby fingers, chuckles and says, "Well, I guess you'd have known for sure what the matter was, if you'd waited just a couple more weeks and felt this baby kick!"

"I'll figure it out when I'm older"

Leslie

MY VERY FIRST MEMORY OF YOU was when Mom told me she was pregnant. We were home from camp, so I think it was September. I remember thinking, Wait! I knew this baby needed a dad, but I didn't want to make Mom sad by asking her how this could happen. I thought to myself, I'll figure it out when I'm older.

Mom said if you were a boy your name would be William. She asked me for suggestions for girls' names. I was very into *Little Women* at that time, and I wanted to name you Elizabeth, or Beth. But Mom said we needed to choose a name that would be easy for you to spell. She was sure she had damaged you by living on black coffee for the first three months of pregnancy. So we decided on Amy, and Elizabeth became your middle name.

Thanksgiving 1958,
Westfield, New Jersey

Ruth

ON THANKSGIVING, WE DRIVE TO Newington to have dinner with Don and Leota and the kids. Winnie is gone for the week, visiting her mother in Philadelphia, and I think we are all glad to have a break from each other. As helpful as it is to have her living with us, and as much as we need the bit of extra money she pays for her room and board, it's not always easy.

It hadn't occurred to me that Winnie, an unmarried woman with no children of her own, would have so many opinions about how mine should be raised, and would feel so free to share them. And I don't think it had occurred to her just how much of a change it would be, moving from a spare and quiet two-room apartment to a rambling two-and-a-half-story house filled with a big family, with all of its commotion and clutter, and its grief.

She moved in at the beginning of August, when the lease on her apartment was up, while we were away in Maine. It was a relief, on our return, to find the lawn mowed, the flowerbeds carefully tended, the refrigerator stocked with food. It was less welcome, over the next few days, to see the small changes she had made throughout the house without consulting me: my reading chair moved to a different corner of the living room, the shelves in the linen closet rearranged. It took me weeks to remember that she had moved the silverware to a drawer to the left of the sink, instead of the right.

Within a couple of months, we had all begun to figure out how to live together. I had learned to pick my battles: the silverware stayed where she had put it, but I dragged my chair back where it belonged.

I saw Steve's face darken when Winnie reprimanded any of the boys for something they had done—leaving a banana peel on the counter, tracking in mud—but he never talked back to her. They were such good kids, and there was so little they did that needed correcting, that I wished she would just let the little things go. But I didn't say anything.

I didn't know how Winnie would react when I came home from the doctor with the news. I half expected that the thought of a new baby in the house—five children!—would be too much, that she would tell me she would look for a new place. But she surprised me.

"Oh, Ruth!" she cried, hugging me fiercely. "Isn't it wonderful? Isn't it a miracle?"

And I had to agree. After the first moments of shock—of thinking about how I would tell the kids, of the unbearable thought that people would pity me even more than they already did, of asking myself how I could possibly cope with raising Bill's child from infancy without him—the feeling I had, even as I left Dr. Hatch's office, was one of sudden, immense gratitude, of wonder. As I walked, still dazed, to the car, I wasn't even surprised to hear Bill's voice, tinged with amusement.

"Just in case you needed something to remember me by, I guess," he said.

Now, two months later, I've gained back most of the weight I lost over the summer, and my pregnancy is obvious. I'd given away all the maternity clothes I wore when I was expecting Leslie years earlier, of course, so I've sewn myself two or three shapeless sacks from the cheapest wash-and-wear fabric I could find, and one nicer dress for church and special occasions. I'm wearing that one today, a dark green wool that flares from the shoulders, concealing my shape without swallowing me up.

When I step through the door into the tumult of Leota's kitchen, she hugs me, and I feel the firm bulge of my belly press against her own flat abdomen. She takes a step back and looks at me appraisingly.

"You look good, Ruth. You've got some color back."

The day is filled with delicious food and good conversation, and laughter, so much laughter. I realize how much I've missed it. The kids laugh with their cousins as they set the table. Leota and I laugh together in the kitchen. Don tells a funny story at dinner, and we all roar with laughter.

It is already getting dark when I gather up the kids for the long drive home. Leota sends us with enough leftovers for days. Don walks me to the car, and our goodbye is a bear hug that lasts for long moments. When he pulls away to look at me, his eyes are wet.

I touch his cheek. "I'm okay," I say. "We're all okay."

Winter 1958–1959

From the Diaries of Leon G. White, Bangor, Maine

Monday, December 22: 12 degrees below this am. Left at 6:20 pm for N.J. to spend Xmas with Ruth and family.

Tuesday, December 23: Arrived at Ruth's at about 10:30 am. Had a nice trip on train, taxi and bus.

Wednesday, December 24: Visiting with Ruth and the children.

Thursday, December 25: Had a nice Christmas with Ruth and the children.

Friday, December 26: Still with Ruth.

Saturday, December 27: Still with Ruth.

Sunday, December 28: Went to church with Ruth and children. Nice sermon. Beautiful church.

Monday, December 29: Still with Ruth.

Tuesday, December 30: Still with Ruth.

Wednesday, December 31: Still with Ruth. Andy's birthday – cake and all the fixings.

Thursday, January 1: Ruth and family brought me to Bridgeport. We all had lunch there and I took train for Hartford, arriving about 3 pm. Donald and Leota met me at station (Berlin, not Hartford).

Friday, January 2: Hartford to Boston on bus – to Bangor on train. Arrived in snowstorm at 7pm. My car was at station. Gilbert had it there.

Christmas 1958, Westfield, New Jersey

Ruth

TRUE TO HIS WORD, MY FATHER arrives in Westfield two days before Christmas, after taking an overnight train from Bangor to Bridgeport, then the bus, which gets in around mid-morning. Leslie and I drive to the station to pick him up, and when he sees me, he looks momentarily surprised, as if he's forgotten about the baby I am carrying. His hug is brief, and a little stiff, but a hug nonetheless.

I settle him into the sunroom, which still contains the bed, nightstand, and dresser we set up there for Lena in another lifetime—was it only last year? I suggest that he might like to lie down after the long trip, but he is restless. He wanders through the house, looking into all of the rooms, making me glad I took the time to tidy everything up, even the spaces, like my sewing room, that I don't usually expect anyone to see.

He asks the boys to show him the large open attic where they sleep, which I hope isn't too messy. I rarely ascend into their domain these days, finding it taxing enough, with my pregnancy well into its third trimester, to go up and down the single flight of stairs to the second floor.

Eventually he settles into a chair at the table in the kitchen, where Leslie and I are baking gingerbread men. Under my supervision, she rolls out the dough, presses the cookie cutter into it, and carefully slides each unbaked cookie onto a baking sheet.

"You can help if you want, Grampa," she says. "Just put on the raisins for the eyes and mouth and buttons, like this."

We move on to spritz cookies next, packing the dough into the metal cookie press and making dozens of buttery stars, wreaths, and Christmas trees, which my father and Leslie decorate painstakingly with colored sugar and cinnamon candies.

I think this may be the first time my father has ever participated in any sort of baking, or, really, any cooking at all, except, when I was a child, during my parents' annual fall tradition of making mincemeat, when his job was to run the venison, suet, and raisins through the grinder before my mother canned it for pies.

The gingerbread men come out of the oven, and Leslie instructs him to use the spatula to slide them carefully onto a cooling rack. When one of them loses a leg, she says, "Don't worry, Grampa, that one can be a try-cake."

When I was very young, my mother baked cakes to order for people in the neighborhood. As she poured the batter into the pans, she made sure to fill one cup of a muffin tin to bake alongside the layers. When it was baked, she called Shume, Don, and me to the kitchen. It was our job to sample the "try-cake," and one we all took very seriously, each of us nibbling a third of the tiny cake slowly, evaluating it for texture and taste.

"You never know," my mother would say, "I might have mixed up the sugar and the salt," but of course she never had.

When the kids come downstairs on Christmas morning and see the packages piled under the tree, it's clear that the boys are surprised. They know money is tight now, and they haven't been expecting to receive much in the way of wants this year, only needs—winter boots and jackets, things I would have had to buy for them anyway. New socks and toothbrushes in their stockings, with an orange in the toe.

Back in the fall, Leslie had become enchanted with a lifelike white plush kitten in the window of a toy store we passed by on a shopping trip downtown and said she hoped Santa Claus would bring her one just like it. It was all she could talk about whenever the subject of Christmas came up. I'd gone back to the store alone one day, but when I saw the price tag, I balked. I couldn't justify spending so much on a toy when there were so many other things she really needed.

Then, during the first week of December, the mailman brought a Christmas card from Bill's old boss at Pratt and Whitney Machine Tool, Whiff Bancroft, and his wife, Elsie. When I opened the envelope, a check fell out, with a note.

"Ruth," it said, "we think of you and your family so often, and know this first holiday season without Bill will be hard for all of you. Please use this check to help the children have a nice Christmas."

I was stunned by the amount—nearly as much as Bill's weekly salary—and my first instinct was to send it right back, to say I couldn't accept such a generous gift. I sat down at my writing desk and reached for an envelope and notepaper, but before I could pick up a pen, I heard Bill's voice.

"Don't, Ruth. They want you to have it for the kids. They want to make Christmas a little easier for you, a little better for all of you. You keep that money, and spend it on something foolish that the kids don't need. Something that will make them happy."

So, instead, I wrote Whiff and Elsie a thank-you note, with the ink a little smudged where a tear had fallen on the paper as I folded it to put it in the envelope.

Breakfast first, with the kids' stockings at the table, before any of the packages under the tree can be opened; that's the way we've always done it. Tradition. Andy pokes at his stocking, grinning when he feels the familiar shape of the orange in the toe. Tradition.

They each find the usual package of socks, the new toothbrush. A small box of ribbon candy. Then, before they get to the orange, each of them draws out a small white box tied with a red ribbon. Steve looks at me questioningly.

"Go ahead and open them," I say. "Leslie first."

She pulls the end of the ribbon to untie it, lifts the lid of the box, and finds a small pink collar with a bell attached. Puzzled, she holds it up.

"Do you think Santa Claus gave me this for Lucky?" she asks. "But it looks too small for him, and it's pink, and Lucky is a boy."

"I don't know," I say. "Maybe it's to go with another present under the tree."

"Ohhh!" she says, her eyes wide.

One by one, the boys open their boxes, and inside, each finds a red Swiss Army knife, engraved with their initials so they won't mix them up. Steve and Greg look at me in surprise—they know these knives are expensive—but I just smile.

"Those look just like the one Daddy used to carry in his pocket!" I say, as if I'm seeing them for the first time.

Andy is already fiddling with his knife, opening the various blades and attachments and admiring each one, and my father is watching him intently, sure he'll slice his finger before he's had the thing for five minutes.

"You be careful with that," he says. "You mother doesn't want to spend Christmas at the emergency room with you."

He probably doesn't remember that each of my brothers received a pocketknife for his eighth birthday, and he almost certainly didn't know how often the housekeeper or I had to tape up a cut finger. Stitches were rarer, but they were needed at least a time or two.

I was never given a knife for my birthday, of course. Since June, Bill's pocketknife has been tucked in the bottom of my jewelry box, beside his gold cufflinks and his Sigma Phi Sigma pin, but now I think maybe I'll start carrying it in my own pocket. It will come in handy, especially when we get to Maine for the summer.

Under the tree, the boys discover two packages addressed to all three of them. Inside one, they find a transistor radio; now they can listen to the Red Sox, or rock and roll, wherever they go. The other box is a deluxe chemistry set. It's something they had talked about with Bill, and something he would surely have lobbied for this year at Christmas. I would have argued that they'd probably blow up the house, or at least burn holes in the table with it, but Bill would have won out, promising to teach them some safety rules about chemicals before they started using it. It will be up to me to do that now.

"This one has my name on it, Mommy!" Leslie says, holding up a square box. "It's from Santa."

"Open it!" I say, and she does, ripping the paper off, nearly shaking with excitement.

"My kitten!" she cries. "My kitten, my kitten, my kitten!"

She cradles the white stuffed kitten to her chest, and her eyes are shining.

"Thank you," I whisper, too softly for anyone but Bill to hear.

"What did I tell you?" he says. "Something foolish, to make her happy."

"A life built around silent mourning to protect the rest of us"

Greg, Andy, Leslie, Amy

Andy: I have been pleasantly surprised to learn that Grampa was so supportive of Mom during the year after Dad died. My impression was that they had a distant, not particularly warm relationship. She would talk about how difficult life was growing up, with his long trips to the woods when he worked for Great Northern Paper Company. And I had the impression that Mom and her brothers did not always have good relationships with the housekeepers Grampa hired to be with the kids when he was off North.

Amy: Almost all of my memories of Grampa are of visiting him in Bangor. I do remember him coming to camp, where he was always very nervous about us being in the lake—I think Mom said it was because he had never learned to swim—and would sit on the deck, clutching the railing, and watch us like a hawk.

The old railing on the deck had one joint that was reinforced with an old license plate, and I remember being told that on one of Grampa's visits, it bothered him that the railing was wobbly, and he had the plate in the trunk of his car and used it to try to make the railing sturdier.

Andy: When Grampa came to the lake he was as you said, kind of worried and judgmental of the freedom Mom allowed us in boats, swimming, etc. He told us more than once that if we ran our outboard motor at half-speed we'd use a lot less gas. Really? Like that was advice we'd take to heart!

Greg: I woke up with another Grampa memory, one from a Newington visit. We boys often went out back of the house a few streets to where land had not been developed, to play. There was a hillside, perhaps a former quarry for highway materials, that we called "the roly-poly rocks." It was a challenge to scramble up the loose stone hillside.

During Grampa's visit, he took us there on a jaunt, and we climbed up, probably around the edge of the steepest part. On the way down, I fell and caught myself with a broken tree branch, in the process stabbing my hand between thumb and forefinger. I remember I cried a lot and Grampa pretty much told me to quit acting like a baby.

After he left for home, I developed an infection and was taken to the doctor. The doctor removed about twenty splinters and administered antibiotics. I distinctly remember thinking that my crying was justified and Grampa was wrong to call me a baby.

Amy: I remember Mom saying that after Dad died, Grampa wanted her to move back to Bangor, but she never really considered it. I always felt that after her mother died, her childhood in Bangor was quite unhappy, and their house was often a sad place to be. I remember her telling me how surprised and grateful she was when, after she got a scholarship to the University of Maine at her high school graduation, Grampa told her that meant there would be enough money for her to live on campus instead of at home. "I felt like I had been set free," she said.

Many of my memories of Grampa involve him fretting about something, although I also remember him lifting me up to pet his deer head hat rack, taking me for walks to the park, and making croquet wickets out of coat hangers so we could play in his backyard.

I can only remember him visiting us in Milford once, but I have such a clear memory of sitting beside him on the couch in the living room; we were reading a book, and he was pointing to words and asking me if I knew what they were, which, I remember, I mostly did. I'm pretty sure that must have been at Christmastime the year before I turned four, and from then on, it seemed to me, suddenly I could read. I used to tell people that my grandfather had taught me to read. I'm sure that made Mom roll her eyes, since she had been reading and pointing out the words to me every day forever.

Leslie: I went to live with Grampa after school was done in May of 1970, after my junior year at the University of Maine. Mom gave me her green Ford Fairlane because I was saving money by living with Grampa, and because I would need transportation to the elementary school where I would be student teaching in the fall. I took summer classes so that I could graduate a semester early and worked at Miller's Restaurant in downtown Bangor evenings. I remember working in Grampa's dining room one evening on a lesson plan that involved a piece of music. I was whistling the notes to try to figure out the melody when I heard Grampa in the kitchen remark to Kathleen how amazed he was that I could whistle a tune from a sheet of music. It didn't seem all that difficult to me, but I did feel proud that he had noticed.

Andy: Much later, when Grampa developed dementia and had to be put in a nursing home, I drove Mom to Bangor to visit him. She would not let me go inside, but went in on her own. When she came out she was distraught—he had not known who she was at all.

As we drove down the turnpike toward home, she was quiet for a long time and when I turned to look at her she was silently crying, tears running down her face. Even then I recall thinking it was the first time I'd seen her physically express such sad heartache. A small opening in the stoicism Mom held to despite the hard losses in her life. The grief for her mother, Dad, her father had to have seemed too much. But we all know Mom—she took deep breaths, dried her tears, and tucked that grief away in the deep recesses of her heart where she could visit it in private whenever she felt the need. A life built around silent mourning to protect the rest of us.

March 2, 1959, Westfield, New Jersey
Ruth

AFTER BREAKFAST, I SHOO LESLIE AND the boys out the door for school, check my watch, and hurry upstairs to take a shower before my appointment. As the warm water runs over my swollen belly, I feel the baby move. The sensation is no longer the light flutter I first felt months earlier, or even the roiling, rolling motion I had grown used to feeling until these last few weeks.

This movement is a slow, steady pressure in one spot, as something—an elbow? a knee?—presses into my abdomen. It is as if the child is deliberately spreading its limbs, trying to make more space in the watery capsule that encloses it, the way my older children poke their bedclothes up to create a private room in which to read by flashlight when they should be sleeping.

I feel the strong wall of muscle yield only slightly to the pressure, can see the rounded bulge—a knee, I think—that forms like a knot on my right side, just above my hip. I know that the baby has dropped, ready to be born. I didn't need the doctor to tell me so at last week's appointment; I have felt it lodged against my pubic bone, pressing against my bladder, for ten days or more.

They call it "lightening," and it's true I can breathe better, can feel the space that has opened up just below my breastbone, letting me fill my lungs completely for the first time in months. But no woman who has experienced it would ever have used that word to describe the sensation of heaviness in the pelvis and lower back that keeps me awake at night and makes every outing an ordeal as I search for the closest parking spaces and calculate the distance between public bathrooms.

I turn the water off, draw back the shower curtain, and reach for the towel rod to steady myself before stepping from the tub and wrapping myself in a bath towel that barely meets around my girth.

I cross the hall to the bedroom—mine alone now—and dress quickly in one of the shapeless sacks I have grown so tired of wearing, topping it with a cardigan sweater I haven't been able to button since before Christmas.

The morning rush is over, traffic light, so the short drive to Dr. Hatch's office is uneventful. After using the restroom, I take a seat in the waiting room and I am relieved when the nurse calls my name almost immediately.

The doctor's examination is gentle, if perfunctory. There is nothing to indicate that labor is imminent, although, by his calculations, my due date is nearly three weeks past.

I remind him that, in four previous pregnancies, I went into labor only once without medical induction, with my second child, Greg, and he was nearly a month overdue before my contractions began.

"They don't come until they're good and ready, do they?" Dr. Hatch observes cheerfully, but I have something I need to say.

Taking a deep breath, I begin. "Doctor. My husband died on June sixteenth."

"A terrible loss," he says, shaking his head sadly, and I remember his kindness to me that night, and his own sorrow.

"Today is March second," I continue. "It has been eight and a half months. If I don't have this baby soon, people will start to talk."

The doctor looks startled, then nods slowly.

"I understand," he says. "Perhaps it's time to give nature a nudge."

"Please," I say. "The sooner the better."

We settle on that very evening; he will meet me at the hospital after his office hours are done for the day. Before the night is over, he says, I'll hold my baby in my arms.

I leave his office, relieved but nervous. It has been nearly ten years since I've had a baby. All of my others were delivered at Hartford Hospital, all within six years, all by the same doctor, who had come to seem almost like a family friend. Even the obstetrical nurses remembered me by the time I returned for the fourth time to give birth to Leslie.

I'll be at a different hospital this time, and surely, in a decade, many things will have changed. Instead of simply breaking the amniotic sac, the doctor has told me, he'll be administering an injection that will start contractions that may be forceful and pain-ful. I'm not afraid of pain, but I don't like not knowing exactly what will happen.

At home, I check the contents of the bag I packed weeks ago and phone Winnie at work to let her know I'll be leaving for the hospital at five.

I want to drive myself, and I tell Winnie there's no reason I can't—I'm not yet in labor, after all—but she is insistent. She'll leave work early, start dinner for the kids, and drive me to the hospital.

I make a list of the things I need to do before going to the hospital: laundry, vacuuming, checking the contents of the freezer to let Winnie know what to make for dinner for the next several nights. I ought to bake a batch of cookies for the kids' school lunches and bring the meatloaf up from the basement freezer to defrost. I should call my brother Don to let him know. I should work my way through the mending basket, sew on the missing buttons and stitch up the ruptured seams, so the kids won't run out of school clothes.

But I make a cup of tea and sit down, instead, to wait.

"I was so proud to be your big sister"
Greg, Andy, Leslie

Greg: I don't have clear and poignant memories of your birth week; sorry. I was in eighth grade in the brand new Edison Junior High. I could meet with friends and bike to school, and I do have some memories of school stuff.

I suppose I was doing extra chores–that's what I did–during the end of Mom's pregnancy. I don't remember any trauma around her going to the hospital or bringing you home.

You know the story of "we have to give the kid a simple name because all my living on black coffee likely will result in brain damage."

Leslie: The neighbors gave Mom a baby shower, and there were lots of little outfits, rattles, and things. No Pampers–they weren't invented yet!

Andy: I think Winnie went to the hospital with Mom. What I recall is her coming up to the attic to tell Greg and me in our "bedroom" that we had a baby sister and she and Mom were both doing fine. It was dark in our room and I remember sitting bolt upright in bed. I don't recall what happened after that—did Greg and I talk about your birth? Probably not. Did we get up or go back to sleep? Steve was in high school—was he at the hospital? Not likely; it was the '50s.

Leslie: I don't remember Mom going to the hospital. I do remember Winnie saying you were a girl, with blonde curls. I was thrilled! I loved my brothers, but I *really* wanted a sister!

Greg: I don't think we boys did a lot of diaper changing and babysitting until you were a bit older. I was not mature enough to take on unsupervised meal prep. I'm sure we all had duties, but all under close supervision. How did Mom manage that household?

Andy: Mom must have spent a couple of days in the hospital before bringing you home in a cardboard "crib." I remember thinking how tiny you were and how amazing it was that you could nap cozily in a box!

Leslie: I don't think I went to see you in the hospital; I think visitors had to be twelve. I remember big pink ribbons on our door, and I wore one to school, probably the day after you were born. When you and Mom came home lots of neighbors came to visit, with baby girl gifts and casseroles. Lots of activity at the Wight house. I was so proud to be your big sister!

March 29, 1959, Westfield, New Jersey

Ruth

WHEN I AWAKEN ON EASTER SUNDAY, Leslie is standing beside my bed, so quietly that I think it must have been the light from the window that woke me, not her presence.

"Mommy," she whispers, when she sees my eyes open, "can I tiptoe downstairs and see if the Easter Bunny came?"

I nod and smile, remembering how the boys, hiding jelly beans last night before they went to bed, made it into a game, challenging each other to find the best hiding places. I suspect we'll be finding jelly beans for weeks.

After the kids were all in bed, I brought four baskets up from the basement and filled them with excelsior and speckled malted milk eggs, topping each one off with a chocolate rabbit and a new yo-yo. The boys might be too old for the Easter Bunny, but not for chocolate and yo-yos.

Then I pulled out the pieces of fabric for what should have been Leslie's new Easter dress and considered, briefly, whether I had the energy to stay up and try to get it done for her to wear to church the next morning. She and I had picked out the material a month ago, when bolts of spring fabrics first appeared in the

stores—a pale green cotton with tiny pink flowers—and I had let
her choose delicate rose-pink buttons that looked as if they had
been made from the inside of a conch shell.

Now I wonder what I was thinking, imagining that I'd find time
to make her a new dress after the baby arrived. In the nine and a
half years since Leslie was born, I'd somehow forgotten what it
was like to have a new baby in the house. Between making up bottles and washing loads of diapers, there seemed to be barely
enough time left over to fix meals, run the vacuum cleaner, and
keep up with the rest of the laundry.

And, I had to admit, I was exhausted. Even though Leslie had
been the fourth child born in six years, having her at twenty-nine,
even with three little boys to chase after, was not the same as having a baby at thirty-nine. My back ached from carrying Amy
against my shoulder while I tried to get things done one-handed.
Her weight at birth—ten pounds and three ounces—had surprised
everyone, especially considering that I had weighed barely ten
pounds more at the end of the pregnancy than I had at the start.

I had thought I could use her naptimes to sew, but, more often
than not, when she was tucked into the bassinet next to my bed
and sleeping soundly, I would lie down for just a minute's rest, and
wake up an hour or two later, when she began to stir.

"It's okay, Mommy," Leslie had said when I told her I didn't
think I could finish her new dress in time for Easter. "It's too cold
for short sleeves anyway," she added, which was true. It had been
the coldest spring we'd experienced since we'd moved to Westfield, and the temperature on Sunday was expected to hover in the
high 30s.

So she would wear the dress I had made for her at Christmas,
a plaid shirtwaist with long sleeves, a high collar, and a full skirt.
Even if it didn't exactly look like spring, at least it matched the
weather, and I was glad she had chosen a more versatile navy and
green plaid, instead of green and red.

It will be our first Easter without Bill, of course, and the first
when we will not travel back to Newington to be with the Baxters
for church and dinner. Instead, we'll go to the church we attend
in Westfield, the church where Winnie works, and where Bill's funeral was held only nine months earlier. We'll come home to our
own Easter dinner, assuming I succeed in setting the timer on the

stove to start it baking the ham and sweet potatoes while we're gone.

This holiday is another milestone in our year of firsts. We've gotten through each of the kids' birthdays, Christmas, my own birthday, Valentine's Day. Soon, I think, in less than three months, we'll no longer be doing all of these things without Bill for the first time. I wonder how it will feel—our second trip to Maine for the summer without him, our second Fourth of July.

Every day, I make plans and decisions Bill and I would once have made together, and, gradually, I am beginning to feel something akin to confidence. In spite of myself, even without a map or a blueprint, somehow I am learning to navigate this new life.

The courage that my mother had
Went with her, and is with her still:
Rock from New England quarried;
Now granite in a granite hill.

The golden brooch my mother wore
She left behind for me to wear;
I have no thing I treasure more:
Yet, it is something I could spare.

Oh, if instead she'd left to me
The thing she took into the grave!-
That courage like a rock, which she
Has no more need of, and I have.

> —Edna St. Vincent Millay,
> "The Courage That My Mother Had"

Spring 1959, Westfield, New Jersey

Ruth

37 MARSHALL ST MILFORD

"What will you do?"

It's the question my father asks me at some point during each of our infrequent phone calls. It's the question I ask myself every night before I fall asleep, and every morning when I wake up. In between, I am too busy to think about it, but the question looms, unspoken, in nearly all of the conversations I have with friends.

It flickers behind Don's dark eyes after he has driven down on a Saturday morning to help us take off the storm windows and put on the screens, and it underlies Reverend McCorison's small talk when we have him and his wife over for dinner one Sunday in April.

Everyone seems to understand that staying where we are is not an option. Westfield isn't home; it's just the place we landed, four years ago, so Bill could take a better job. There's nothing here to hold us now.

Betty and Elmer, and Don and Leota, all wish we would move back to Newington. It's the place that, next to Maine, feels to all of us like the closest thing to home.

My father tells me there's room for all of us in his house in Bangor. He says he can put in a set of bunk beds so that one of the guest rooms will accommodate all three of the boys, and Leslie and I can have the other, with its two high twin beds. No one but us ever stays in them anyway, he says, which is true. Don and Leota stay with her parents when they visit him. Shume and Jerry don't come, and if they ever did, they would surely choose to stay with Gib and Joyce.

The boys have no doubts about what they would do, if I left it up to them.

"Couldn't we move to Bethel?" Greg asks. "Then we'd be close to camp, and we could check on it in the winter and shovel the roof—"

"And walk across the lake on the ice!" Andy says.

Steve doesn't say much. Wherever we go, the move will be hardest on him, starting out in a new school as a high school junior. But I know that, like the other boys, he would choose Bethel in an instant.

It's what I want, too—someday. It's the future Bill and I always planned. But right now, when I envision a life in that "house on a hill in Bethel" that we always talked about, I know the time isn't right. It's too soon for me to imagine myself there without Bill, and what would I find to do in Bethel that might support five children?

It's hard for me to think about going to work, with Amy less than two months old, but eventually, I know, I'll have to find a way to earn some money.

Thankfully, Bill's life insurance allowed me to pay off the mortgage on the house in Westfield. The whole area is growing in popularity—it's both close enough to and far enough from New York City to appeal to young families—and I am hoping that, when I figure out what to do, where to go, I'll be able to sell it for more than I'll have to pay for our next house.

And there are the Social Security survivors benefits checks that come each month, and some money we had been saving for the future—a very different future than the one I need to plan for now. But our biggest asset, I think, is my innate frugality. I won't spend even a nickel unwisely if I can possibly help it, and it gives me a sense of pride to know that, if anyone can figure this out, I can.

The answer comes suddenly, unexpectedly, on a Friday evening in early May. Winnie returns home from work and announces that she has accepted a job as the Christian education director at the Orange Congregational Church in Orange, Connecticut.

I know she has been looking to move on from the Westfield church, where she has been the associate director of Christian education for eight years. She has already applied for several director positions without being hired, but she seemed to have settled into the idea of staying where she was for the time being.

"Will you find an apartment?" I ask.

"I was thinking that maybe we could all move there together," she says, with a note of hesitation in her voice that is unusual for her. She pulls a highway map from her purse and unfolds it.

"Look, Ruth. Orange is only forty miles from Newington. You could go to see your brother's family, and Betty, as often as you wanted."

I study the map. Orange is right on the Wilbur Cross Parkway, a section of Route 15, the same route we've taken each time we've made the drive to Newington from Westfield. It would be an easy drive of less than an hour, one we could do on Saturday mornings, or Sundays after church.

And we'd be a hundred miles closer to Maine.

The next few weeks are a flurry of activity. Leaving Amy home with Winnie, the older kids and I make two quick trips to Orange, two Saturdays in a row, to look at houses with a real estate agent whose name and number I find by calling directory assistance, since we don't know anyone in that area.

On the first trip, the boys fall in love with a huge old house in Orange. It has five bedrooms and a yard with trees and gardens and enough space to play baseball or croquet. They walk through the rooms, talking enthusiastically among themselves, but all I can see, as the agent shows us around, is how much work the house will need. The roof is in need of new shingles, the kitchen appliances are dated, and the plumbing has seen better days. A year ago, I might have been excited, too, at the prospect of working together, all of us, to make the house our own. Now just the thought of all that work makes me weary.

I tell the boys I'm sorry, but we just can't buy a "fixer-upper." I don't add "now that we don't have Daddy to fix it up," but they nod; they understand the reason.

On our next trip, the real estate agent wants to show us a house in an adjacent town, Milford, that she thinks will be perfect for us.

"It's a Cape Cod," she tells me, her voice animated, "and it's on a large lot in a nice neighborhood."

I'm not about to get my hopes up—all the Capes I've ever seen have been far too small for seven people—but I agree to take a look. When we pull into the driveway, I admit that the lot is nice, but I tell her right away that this house won't be big enough for us.

"I think you'll be surprised," she insists, but I don't want to waste her time, or mine.

"How many bedrooms?"

She hesitates. "Well...I think we can call it five."

As it turns out, once we get inside, the house really is a lot bigger than it looks. Downstairs, there's a bedroom that can be Winnie's, a kitchen and dining room that are small but adequate, and a good-sized living room, as well as the only full bathroom.

The second floor is the real surprise. Gable dormers on the front, and a long shed dormer across the entire back, give it far more space than I would have imagined. Two of the upstairs bedrooms, near the top of the stairs, are small, but big enough for Leslie and me. The third, at the end of a hall, is huge; it stretches the entire depth of the house, with windows in both the front and back dormers, and two more windows on the long side of the room. Three twin beds, three desks, and three dressers will fit in this room, with space to spare.

The fourth upstairs "bedroom" is not a bedroom at all, but a walk-in storage closet, no more than six or seven feet square, and painted a ghastly bright pink, the color of Pepto-Bismol. But it does have a window, high up in the shed dormer, and it adjoins the small bedroom I will take.

"We'll make an offer," I tell the agent, before I can change my mind or overthink things.

"This can be Amy's room," I say to the kids.

"I feel bad that we got to see her room before she did," Leslie says, as if a two-month-old would know the difference.

I spend the kids' last few weeks of school sorting through everything that has accumulated in the garage and basement, in the backs of closets and on high cupboard shelves, in the four years we've lived here. I separate what we'll need to take to Maine for the summer and start to pack up as much of the rest as I can. I contact a real estate agent and list the house, which she thinks will sell quickly, and I schedule the movers to come on a Thursday, the day after school gets out.

By the end of that day, we'll be moved into the house in Milford. We'll spend just two nights there, unpacking what we can, packing again for Maine. Then we'll leave it to Winnie, who will be alone in the new house all summer, to do the lion's share of the work of settling in—to finish setting up the kitchen, to open our boxes of books and arrange them in the bookcases, to meet the new neighbors.

I don't stop to question the wisdom of this plan, to wonder if we should spend a little more time getting used to our new home, should delay the trip to Maine by a day, two days, a week.

Because this is what we do: the school year ends, and we head for camp, just as soon as we possibly can.

"We never lingered in transitions; it was get up and go"

Steve, Greg, Andy, Leslie

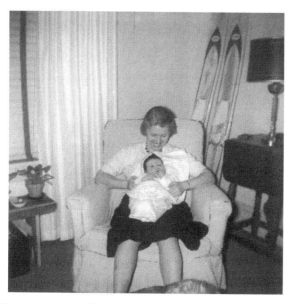

Andy: We moved to Milford with the rationale that it was near to Orange, where Winnie was going to be the church's Christian education director. Mom did not want to move to Bethel (the boys' choice) or to Newington (Betty and Elmer's choice).

There was some brief consideration of moving back to Newington, but it held too many memories for Mom and she said later that she'd have felt out of the loop with all the couples she and Dad knew there. And Mom being Mom, she did not want to be the recipient of any sympathy or pity. She was so hard-headed and tough, determined we could make it on our own.

Greg: I've never really thought about Mom with a months-old baby making the decision to move, house-hunting, buying, selling, moving. I don't remember questioning the decision to move, given that it was not driven by any immediate need. Winnie was clearly her main counselor in all that.

Andy: I remember a couple of trips to Connecticut to look for a house. Steve, Greg, and I liked a big old rambling house in Orange, but Mom knew it needed too much work, so we ended up on Marshall Street in Milford. Not only could she work wonders, she could make up her mind fast and stick with her plan for moving.

Steve: Winnie had moved in with us soon after Dad died. It bothered me greatly that from the time she moved in, she seemed to feel that she had disciplinary rights over us. That probably formed the less than accepting attitude I always had toward her. Our move to Milford was, I'm sure, due in large part to her new job in Orange. I think Mom would have liked to return to Newington, though she did often say that it would never have been the same because she would "feel like a fifth wheel" around her married friends.

Leslie: I don't know exactly when we bought the house in Milford, but I do remember my first day of school there. I had become extremely attached to Mom, to the point where I couldn't make it through the night at a friend's sleepover. I remember trying several times, but by 10 p.m. I was begging to be brought home. School was the same for me. I didn't make it past noon that first day. There were no guidance counselors back in those days—just tough it out.

Andy: When we moved in 1959, I think it was right after school, and since Winnie was involved, we dumped our stuff and ran off to Maine, possibly leaving her to do some settling in. How in the world did we all just return to Milford at the end of the summer and jump into new schools with no friends or known teachers, etc.? One thing is sure—we never lingered in transitions; it was get up and go.

June 20, 1959

Ruth

WHEN WE CROSSED THE BORDER from Massachusetts into New Hampshire, Leslie remarked that she liked the New Hampshire part of the trip best, because it was the shortest. An hour and a half in Connecticut, two and a half in Massachusetts, but only a half hour—twenty minutes, really—to cross the narrow southeast corner of New Hampshire. The last two hours, one on the Maine Turnpike and one on Route 26, the narrow two-lane north from Gray, will take us all the way to the turn for camp.

Bill always quoted from *The Legend of Sleepy Hollow* when we crossed this bridge into Maine. Now, as the car rumbles over the first set of metal expansion plates and onto the deck of the bridge, I sense that the kids are watching me, waiting, wondering if I'll say the words, or if this family tradition is one that died with their father a year ago. It comes to me all at once that I didn't say the words when we crossed the bridge last year, that I never even thought about them. Truthfully, I can't remember much about either of those drives to Maine last June, or the trip back to New Jersey in between.

Now I draw a breath and break the silence. My voice sounds shaky, but loud, to my own ears: "Once you cross that bridge, my friend..."

The kids sit up straight then, as if waking suddenly from a long sleep, and, after a pause, they shout with me, all four of them together: "The ghost is through—his power ends!" Leslie's voice rises to a triumphant squeal on the last word, but the boys let their voices drop low, recalling their father's dramatic whisper. I feel a catch in my throat, and when I look at their faces in the rear-view mirror, their eyes are wide. I see tears on Andy's cheeks, but when he catches my eye in the mirror, he turns his head to the window and shrugs to wipe them away with the shoulder of his T-shirt.

Their raised voices startle the baby, and she fusses a little, but quiets again when Greg shakes a rattle above her and makes a face, wiggling his ears and sticking out his tongue until she smiles. I'm surprised to realize that I'm smiling, too.

We're back in Maine. The camp–our camp, Bill's camp–is waiting for us, with windows to be thrown open, blankets to air, and a winter's accumulation of cobwebs and mouse droppings to be swept away. The summer stretches before us, shimmering and indistinct, like the highway in the sun.

Afterword

Andy

I FIND MYSELF THINKING ABOUT the night at age six, when roused by Mom at 11 p.m. to see my first eclipse of the moon. Just the two of us, sitting by the second floor back bedroom window of our Newington house, looking up at the night sky. As the earth's shadow slowly curved across the beacon moon, she held a piece of white paper on the sill to dramatize that darkening. Gently explaining the alignments of moon, earth, and sun creating soft fading then return of light, she emphasized its wondrous rarity in our lives.

Rare alignment. In many ways that describes my relationship with Mom. Held together by unbreakable forces, orbiting about each other (Mother Earth, Son Moon?): I pulling centrifugally against her inescapable centripetal bonds; she observing with degrees of dismay the apogees and perigees of filial affection.

But held, nonetheless, unceasingly in the mysterious, inexplicable grace-filled ties which not even death can undo.

For years I privately felt Dad's absence with sadness and longing. It underlay my adolescence and early adulthood. Then the "magic" started. He suddenly appears to me—shadowy but present, mostly when I am in a stuck place—frustrated, anxious, angry at myself, lonely, scared, down. Every time, he sits quietly smiling and laughing, as if enjoying seeing me wrestling with my feelings. Never judging or telling me what to do, but his demeanor letting me know that I am okay and he loves me just as I am. I find I can loosen up and laugh at myself along with him.

So his body, his bones, his blood are gone, but he is still alive for me in ways beyond understanding. I'll take that mystery anytime.

Love you, Amy. You know we all think of you in part as Dad resurrected. Birth out of death—talk about miraculous mystery!

You can make me laugh at myself, too.

Acknowledgments

I am grateful to everyone who played a part in getting this book to the finish line, more than sixteen years after I first conceived the idea. In trying to thank them all, I will undoubtedly leave out as many as I include. The more I reflect on how I became a writer, and on how this particular book came to be, the more I understand that my writing has been informed, inspired, and shaped by nearly everyone in my life with whom I have interacted in any meaningful way.

My mother, Ruth White Wight, was the toughest, strongest, most capable person I have ever known. She was practical, reliable, and level-headed. She was also compassionate, generous, and funny. Throughout her life, she was filled with both intellectual curiosity and a sense of wonder. She noticed and appreciated, and shared with her kids, things that other people missed—dewy spider webs at sunrise, the scent of fresh-mown hay, the smooth surface of a pond that was just like glass. These are the qualities for which I most strive myself, and to the extent that I possess any of them, it is because of her.

She was not sentimental, and she brooked no nonsense. Her expressions of pride and words of encouragement to her children were tempered with restraint, but her delight in our accomplishments, and her love for us, were never in doubt. In the words of the late poet Leo Dangel, "She's still moving me to a softer place."

My father, William Walton Wight, could build anything, fix anything, figure anything out. He was born in Oquossoc and raised in Bethel and he was the quintessential Mainer—practical, resourceful, and outdoorsy—until the day he died, even though he spent the last half of his life living in exile in Connecticut and New Jersey.

He died more than eight months before I was born, but my dad's legacy was to remain a vital and immediate part of the family he left behind, during my childhood and beyond—even now, so many decades after his death.

His legacy is in the wooden boat and the family camp, where his musty suede camp jacket still hangs in the loft. It's in the fact that by the time we went to kindergarten we could all identify feldspar, mica, quartz, beryl, tourmaline, and—our favorite because we loved the way it rolled off our tongues—lavender lepidolite. It's in the way none of us is afraid to tackle a building or repair project, confident that we can always figure it out as we go along. It's in the way, over the years, we've all been drawn to the state of Maine—three of us to stay—and the way we all consider Maine our true spiritual home. It's in the way we all love the woods, the water, our kids.

His legacy is in every part of our lives.

I could not have written this book without the help of my brothers, Steve, Greg, and Andy Wight, and my sister, Leslie Wight Grenier. Except for the stories our mom shared with me herself, all of the memories in *Just Like Glass* are theirs, given to me to do with as I wished, without hesitation and with an open-hearted generosity that fills me with so much gratitude and love that sometimes it overflows from my eyes and I find my cheeks wet with it.

Just months before she passed away, my beloved sister-in-law Peggy, our family's BBSE—the Best Big Sister Ever—urged me to "finish that book while we're all still here to read it!" Although I think of those words with regret, I know she would be glad to know that it did, finally, get done. She is always in my heart.

When I began writing this book, my cousin Elaine Grant painstakingly combed through our grandfather's diaries, transcribing all of the entries containing references to my father's death, and to my mother and my siblings during the year that followed, allowing me to add another voice to this family memoir.

Ralph Waldo Emerson wrote, "A friend is a person with whom I may be sincere. Before him, I may think aloud." Donna Funteral, my confidante, champion, cover designer, and so much more, has been my best friend since the second day of second grade. With her, I share six decades of history, and the sense of comfort and security that comes from being truly seen, known, and understood by another person—and being loved anyway. Last spring, I sent her the nearly-completed manuscript of this book, and she read it in a single sitting, because, she said, "Once I started, I wanted to read it all on Mother's Day."

My dear friend Pat Donovan, too, was an early reader of *Just Like Glass*. On hundreds of morning walks by the ponds of Greenwood, we have shared hopes and dreams, frustrations and disappointments, reflections on our forty-five-year friendship, and sweet memories of my mom, who babysat her four boys for many years. "I'm feeling so blessed to have had your mom in my life and my family's," she said when she finished reading. And I am blessed to have her in mine.

Maria Macri is the reason I survived high school and, especially, junior high. She was an inspirational model of nonconformity and creativity in a time and place where those qualities were not widely esteemed. I treasure our lifelong friendship.

Thank you to all of the members of my writing groups, past and present, and to every instructor who helped to improve my writing, beginning with the elementary school teachers who believed me when I said I was going to be an author when I grew up. My junior high English teacher, the late Rick Kravet, taught me to diagram sentences, saw how I took to it, then let me sit in the back of the room and write stories while the rest of the class practiced grammar skills. Jack Saboeiro taught me sophomore biology, but he opened my eyes to philosophy, and to the importance of being kind.

Thank you to the Maine Writers and Publishers Alliance for all of their good efforts in support of writers throughout Maine. I am awed and inspired by the creativity, talent, and determination of the writers in this state, and grateful beyond words to four of the very best—and busiest—contemporary Maine writers. Richard Blanco, Elizabeth Peavey, Bill Roorbach, and Monica Wood all said yes without hesitation when I asked them to read this manuscript and contribute blurbs, and they did so with an open heart and a deep understanding of what I was trying to convey. Thank you. Abrazos.

There is a long list of people, nearly all now gone, who doubtless had no idea of their importance in my life. These are the family, friends, and acquaintances in western Maine who, when I came to this place—my ancestral home—to live, forty years after my father had left it to seek his fortune, and twenty years after he had died, still remembered him.

Our camp neighbors shared tools and visits and garden tomatoes and an occasional helping hand when their camps and ours were being built. Sayward and Cynthia Lamb, Stan and Gertrude Andrews, Brad and Betty Emerson, and Ada Balentine all figure prominently in memories of my childhood. Pete and Joan Seaman became dear friends in later years, when they built the home on the Mann Road where they still live, but Joan's parents, the Proberts, were North Pond fixtures from my family's beginning there.

My Bethel relatives, including my father's aunts Marjorie Cummings and Grace Buck and his cousins Raymond and Albert Buck and their wives, Beatrice and Norma, always regarded us Wights as part of their family. They looked out for my mother in little ways that I noticed, even as a child, giving me the sense of security and belonging that only an extended family can.

Pete Chapin, who ran the Shell station in Bethel, was my father's close friend from their years at Gould Academy. He and his wife, Polly, visited us at camp, and Pete always made sure to change the oil in my mother's car and inspect the brakes before we left Maine at the end of the summer for the long drive back to Connecticut.

In January of 1978, the brothers Brown—John, Don, and Edwin—and Edwin's wife, Musa, welcomed me to the offices of the family-owned *Bethel Citizen* for a month-long college independent study project. Under their tutelage, I learned more about the people, places, and history of the Bethel area than I could have any other way. According to Edwin, although they were never caught, it was my father and Pete, along with Herbie Rowe, another childhood friend and frequent co-conspirator, who caused quite a stir one summer night back in the late 1920s, when they tossed some firecrackers around at the Bethel Inn, awakening the guests and blowing a large hole in the golf course.

I am grateful for every memory of my father shared with me by the folks of his hometown, and to all of them for the part they played in making me feel as if I belonged here—even the older woman I met in the hardware store who told me, "I remember your father, and you look like him—he had a round face, too."

Madeline Mary Wynn, known to me always as Auntie Winnie, lived with my family for several years after my father died and remained a family friend for the rest of her life. Her relationships with my mother and siblings were more complicated, but to me, it was simple: I always knew that her pride and love for me were unconditional and forever.

To Tony, love of my life, and our kids, Katie, Annie, Cait, and Will—it would take another whole book to relate the ways in which you have all made life better, richer, more fulfilling, and more fun. Thank you for your love and encouragement. And Will, for being my cheerleader, and my editor and publisher: I owe you a lobster. At the very least.

To all the rest of the many advocates and champions with whom I've been blessed throughout my life, my circle of extended family and friends, and my unwitting mentors: if you cheered me on; if you judged my elementary school essay worthy of an award; if you took the time to leave a comment on my blog; if you took a red pen to a draft of something I wrote, and thereby made me a better writer—thank you. You helped.

About the Author

Despite having been born in New Jersey and raised in Connecticut, Amy Wight Chapman has never really belonged anywhere but in Maine, and she got here as soon as she could. Both of her parents were displaced Maine natives, and she has spent every summer of her life at "camp"—a ramshackle cabin on a small lake in the western Maine foothills. Amy and her husband, Tony, have four adult children. They continue to live at camp during the summer, and spend the remainder of the year just three miles away, in the town of Greenwood.

Made in the USA
Columbia, SC
12 November 2024

46294873R00143